Illustration

Illustration
Index II

Frontispiece
Darrel Anderson/Braid

© Page One Publishing Ptd Ltd
   Block 4 Pasir Panjang Road
   #06-35 Alexandra Distripark
   Singapore 0511
   Tel: (65) 274-3188
   Fax: (65) 274-1833

Distributed worldwide (except Asia) by:

Könemann Verlagsgesellschaft mbH
Bonner Straße 126
D-50968 Köln
Germany

Distributed in Asia by:

Page One The Bookshop Pte Ltd
Block 4 Pasir Panjang Road
#08-33 Alexandra Distripark
Singapore 0511

Designed by Peter Feierabend, Berlin
Layout by K.C. Sin, Singapore
Colour separation by Columbia Overseas Marketing Pte Ltd
Printed by LeeFung-Asco Printers, Hong Kong
Printed in China
ISBN 981-00-6323-7

Contents · Inhalt · Sommaire · Indice

Foreword

Communication shapes our daily lives and extends into every area of our activity. The visual media are multiplying: ever more sophisticated, they continue their advance into our public environment, our offices and our homes. The information they communicate must attract our attention; it must be quick and easy to assimilate, and it must not be boring. Visual components thereby reinforce the message – and are indeed often made the sole vehicle of communication.

For those wishing to harness the power of the visual media, for those seeking to translate a meaningful statement into an equally potent image, there can be no better way than to draw upon the best, most creative experts in the field.

In its Index series, Page One Publishing provides a forum in which leading international photographers, architects, graphic designers, typographers and illustrators can present their work. The user is thereby granted a fascinating overview of a broad range of ideas, styles and working methods. The addresses of all the artists are given at the end of each volume.

There is a separate Index for each branch of the visual media. The present volume, dedicated to illustration, is divided into chapters as diverse as Humour, Animals, Food, Science Fiction, Transport and Architecture.

The books in the Index series are intended not just for potential customers in specialist fields, but also for an interested international public, and not least for creative designers themselves. For them, the Index is both a platform for their work and at the same time a rich opportunity for artistic exchange – a sort of global network for creativity.

Our particular thanks go to the many contributors from all over the world whose remarkable illustrations have enabled us to compile the present book.

Vorwort

Kommunikation bestimmt unseren Alltag, und kein Bereich ist mehr davon ausgeschlossen. Die Medien zur Vermittlung visueller Informationen werden vielfältiger, perfekter und halten weiteren Einzug in Öffentlichkeit, Haushalt oder Büro. Informationen werden vermittelt. Sie sollen Aufmerksamkeit erregen, schnell und einfach erfaßbar sein und nicht langweilen. Die visuelle Komponente betont dabei die Aussage, wird oft zum alleinigen Träger.

Wer sich mit diesen Bereichen auseinandersetzt, wer eine optimale visuelle Umsetzung sucht, ist darauf angewiesen, mit den Kreativsten und Besten zusammenzuarbeiten.

Page One Publishing bietet in seinen Indexen ein Forum, in dem international herausragende Photographen, Architekten, Grafikdesigner, Typographen und Illustratoren sich mit ihren Arbeiten exemplarisch vorstellen. Der Benutzer erhält so eine breite Übersicht über die unterschiedlichsten Ideen, Stile und Arbeitsweisen. Die Adressen am Ende des jeweiligen Index ermöglichen die Kontaktaufnahme.

Jede Sparte erhält einen eigenen Index, der in verschiedene Kapitel gegliedert ist. Der vorliegende Band zum Thema Illustration beinhaltet Arbeiten zu so unterschiedlichen Bereichen wie Humour, Animals, Food, Science Fiction, Transport und Architecture.

Die Index-Bände wenden sich nicht nur an spezialisierte potentielle Auftraggeber, sondern zugleich an ein interessiertes internationales Publikum und nicht zuletzt an die Kreativen selbst. Für sie ist der Index ein Forum zur Darstellung. Er bietet ihnen aber auch die Chance zu einem Austausch untereinander, eine Art weltweites Netzwerk für Kreativität.

Unser besonderer Dank gilt den vielen Einsendern aus aller Welt, die es uns mit ihren außerordentlichen Beiträgen ermöglicht haben diesen Band zum Thema Illustration vorzulegen.

Préface

La communication régit notre quotidien et n'exclut plus aucun domaine. Les médias vecteurs d'informations visuelles deviennent toujours plus variés, se perfectionnent et continuent de s'introduire dans la vie publique, les foyers ou les bureaux. Il y a transmission d'informations. D'informations qui doivent capter l'attention, être saisies rapidement et facilement, ne pas ennuyer l'utilisateur. La composante visuelle souligne le message, en devient même souvent le support exclusif.

Si l'on veut exploiter ces domaines et que l'on aspire à une transcription visuelle optimale, il faut travailler avec les meilleurs auteurs et les plus créatifs.

Dans ses index, Page One Publishing offre un forum idéal aux grands créateurs: photographes, architectes, stylistes graphistes, typographes et illustrateurs de réputation internationale s'y présentent avec des travaux exemplaires. L'utilisateur trouve une large vue d'ensemble sur les idées, les styles et les méthodes de travail les plus divers. A la fin de chaque index figurent les adresses qui permettent de contacter la personne souhaitée.

Il existe un index par catégorie; chacun est divisé en chapitres. Le volume présent, consacré à l'illustration, contient des travaux sur des domaines extrêmement différents, tels que Humour, Animals, Food, Science Fiction, Transport et Architecture.

Les volumes d'index ne sont pas conçus uniquement pour d'éventuels commettants spécialisés; ils s'adressent à un public international intéressé, mais aussi et surtout aux créateurs eux-mêmes. Si l'index est pour eux un forum de présentation personnelle, il leur offre également l'occasion d'échanger des idées et fait fonction de réseau mondial de la créativité.

Nous remercions particulièrement les nombreux créateurs de leurs envois venus du monde entier. C'est grâce à leurs prestations exceptionnelles que nous avons pu réaliser ce volume sur le thème de l'illustration.

Prólogo

La comunicación rige los destinos de nuestra vida diaria; ya no queda ningún ámbito que se excluya a su influencia. Los medios para la trasmisión de informaciones visuales son cada vez más variados y perfectos; se están introduciendo en mayor medida en la vida pública, el hogar y la oficina. Se trasmiten informaciones que han de despertar la atención, permitir apropiarse de ellas de modo rápido y sencillo, y no aburrir. La componente visual subraya el mensaje; frecuentemente se convierte en el único soporte.

Quien se dedica a estos sectores, quien busca una transformación visual ideal, tendrá que colaborar con los más creativos, con los mejores.

Page One Publishing ofrece en sus índices un foro en el que se presentan fotógrafos, arquitectos, diseñadores gráficos, tipógrafos e ilustradores de prestigio internacional, con trabajos ejemplares. De este modo, el usuario obtiene una amplia visión de conjunto sobre las más diferentes ideas, estilos y modos de trabajo. Las direcciones que se ofrecen al final de cada índice facilitan la toma de contacto.

Cada sección tiene su propio índice, dividio en capítulos. El presente volumen, sobre el tema de la ilustración, contiene trabajos sobre ámbitos tan distintos como Humour, Animals, Food, Science Fiction, Transport y Architecture.

Estos volúmenes se dirigen no sólo a potenciales clientes especializados, sino también a un amplio público internacional y a los creativos mismos. Para ellos, es un foro para presentarse; pero también les ofrece la oportunidad de intercambiarse, una especie de red para creativos.

Deseamos expresar nuestro especial agradecimiento a los numerosos remitentes de todo el mundo que, con sus extraordinarios trabajos, nos han permitido realizar este volumen sobre el tema de la ilustración.

Artist
Scott Angle
Title
School Days for DooFus

◁ *Artist*
Scott Angle
Title
Summer Marathon
Client
Listen Magazine

◁◁ *Artist*
Silvio Irilli, A.I. Member
Title
Verso U.S.A. '94
Client
Tuttosport

Artist
Mario Bag
Title
"Chico Buarque" - Brazilian Songwriter

Artist
Mario Bag
Title
Madonna in Brazil
Client
Interview Magazine

Artist
Thomas Cain
Title
Just a Chiquita

Artist
Mario Bag
Title
The Tax Collector
Client
Interview Magazine

Artist
Leland Klanderman,
Ceci Bartels Associates
Client
McMillan Carpet

Artist
Mario Bag
Title
"World Cup '94" - Record Cover
Client
Som Livre Records

Artist
Kazushige Nitta,
David Goldman Agency
Title
The Conductor

Artist
Jeanne Brunnick
Title
Whoops
Client
MSK Advertising

Artist
Scott Angle
Title
Mad Hacker

Artist
Scott Angle
Title
His Airness
Client
Listen Magazine

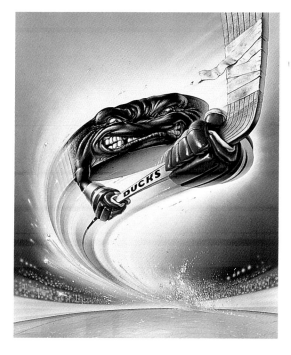

Artist
Francisco Rodriguez Maruca,
Ceci Bartels Associates
Client
Cloverleaf

Artist
Justin Carroll,
Ceci Bartels Associates
Title
Mighty Ducks
Client
Touchstone Pictures

Artist
Leslie Bates
Title
Fred Astaire

Artist
Justin Carroll,
Ceci Bartels Associates
Title
Zulu Surf
Client
Paper Moon Graphics

Artist
Leslie Bates
Title
The Clown

Artist
Justin Carroll,
Ceci Bartels Associates
Title
Good N Fruity

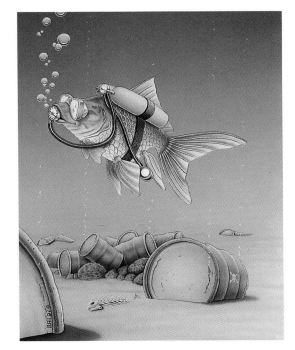

Artist
Leslie Bates

Artist
Kazushige Nitta,
David Goldman Agency
Title
Business Forecast

Artist
James A. Durk

Artist
Jeanne Brunnick
Title
Home for Summer Vacation
Client
Mountain Bell Telephone

Artist
James A. Durk
Title
Fast Food

Artist
Robbie Short
Title
Palace Guard
Client
Bell South

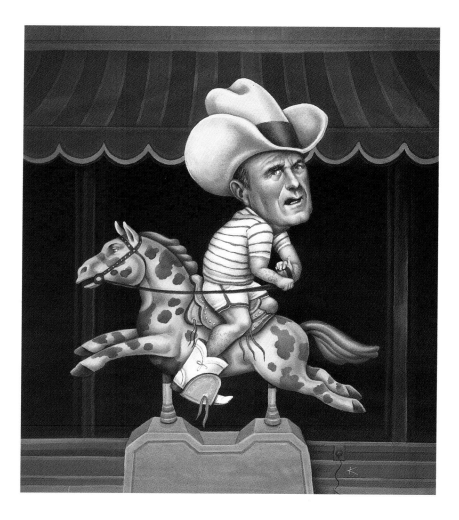

Artist
Eric White
Title
Demi Moore in
the Scarlet Letter
Client
Entertainment Weekly

(top left)
Artist
Anita Kunz
Title
George Bush
Client
Texas Monthly Magazine

(bottom left)
Artist
Anita Kunz
Title
An Article about Baboons
Client
Discover Magazine

(top right)
Artist
Anita Kunz
Title
Chuck Berry
Client
Rolling Stone Magazine

(bottom right)
Artist
Anita Kunz
Title
Little Steven
Client
Rolling Stone Magazine

Artist
Mauro Evangelista,
A.I. Member
Title
Mr. Muscle

Artist
Mauro Evangelista,
A.I. Member
Title
The Human Cannonballs

Artist
Robbie Short
Title
Playhouse
Client
Georgia-Pacific Corp.

Artist
Peter Pijak

Artist
Roger De Muth
Title
Santa Claws
Client
De Muth Design

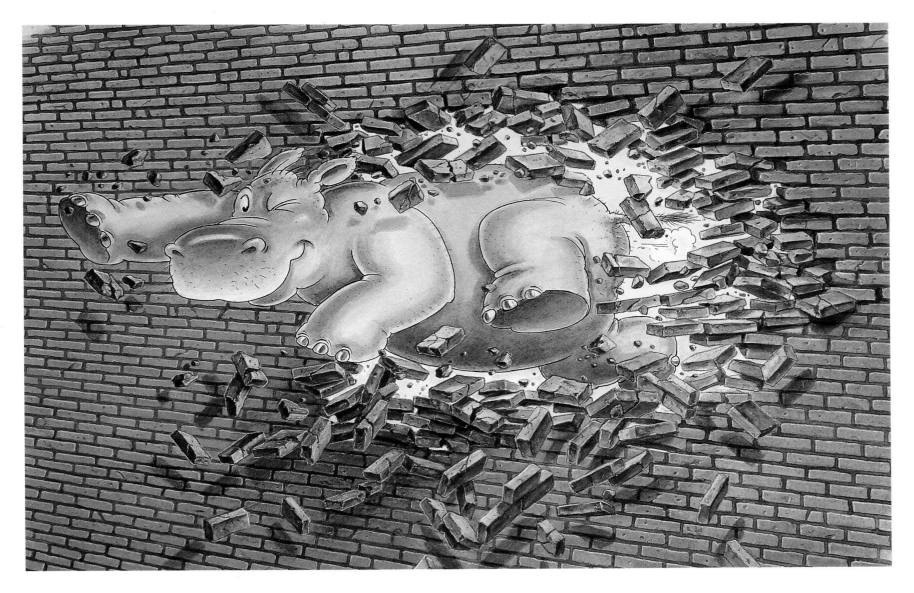

Artist
Mario Kessler
Title
Advertising Figure for
Phamaceutical Product
Client
Holzapfel, Boeving & Partner

Artist
Mario Kessler
Title
Legendary Bavarian Figure
"Wolpertinger"
Client
Freework

Artist
Eric White
Title
Andy Warhol's Secret Desire to
rejoin his Idol, Walt Disney
Client
Mondo 2000

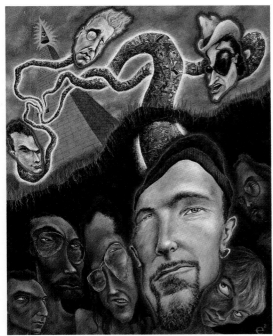

Artist
Eric White
Title
U2 vs Negativland
Client
Mondo 2000

▷ *Artist*
Eric White
Title
American Being
Client
The City Magazine

Artist
Don Weller,
The Weller Institute for the Cure of Design
Title
The Pitbull and the Mountain Goat Illustration
Client
Park City Lodestar Magazine

Artist
Abe Gurvin
Title
Don't Fall Prey
Client
Fotoyhi-Alonso Advertising

Artist
Abe Gurvin
Title
Sometimes the Risks are Hidden
Client
IVAX Corporation

(top right)
Artist
Lindy Burnett,
Ceci Bartels Associates

Artist
Peter Pijak

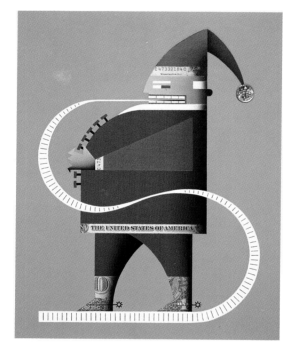

Artist
Jeanne Brunnick
Title
The Adventures of Indiana Bones
Client
Richmond / Sheppard Advertising

Artist
Abe Gurvin
Title
Red Robin Menu
Client
Red Robin Restaurants

Artist
James Yang,
David Goldman Agency
Title
Barber Mouse
Client
Washington Post Magazine

Artist
Lisa Manning
Title
Repeated Repetition

Artist
James A. Durk
Title
Busy Bee

Artist
Lisa Manning
Title
Santa

Artist
Davide Bressan
Title
Starry Night
Client
Work Inedit

Artist ▷
Geoffrey Moss,
Marion Moskowitz Represents Inc.
Title
Diversity vs Tradition /
The Politically Correct Debate
Client
George Washington University

Artist
Valeria Petrone,
A.I. Member
Title
Little Fearless John

Artist
Waleed Shaalan

Artist
Peter Pijak

Artist
Dan Yaccarino
Title
Fall Harvest

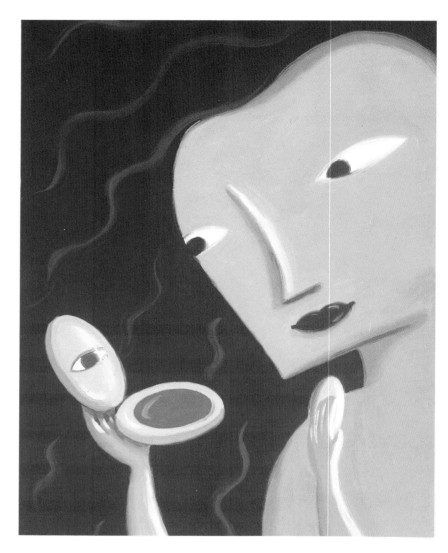

Artist
Dan Yaccarino
Title
Girl with Compact
Client
Le Monde

Artist
Dan Yaccarino
Title
How the Mighty have fallen
Client
South Florida Magazine

Artist
Dan Yaccarino
Title
Girl with Fishbowl
Client
Paper Moon Graphics

Artist
Peter Clark
Title
Yuppie Car Boot

(bottom left)
Artist
Darius Detwiler,
Dick Washington Artists' Rep.
Title
Rain 94
Client
1995 Workbook

(bottom right)
Artist
Aletha Reppel
Title
Tipping
Client
Texas Restaurant Association

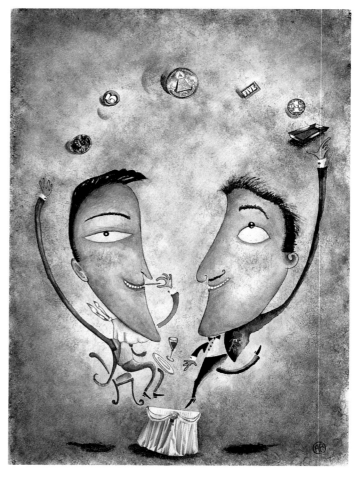

Artist
Peter Clark
Title
Fun Fiddler

(bottom left)
Artist
Darius Detwiler,
Dick Washington Artists' Rep.
Title
Zoo 94
Client
National Advertising Market

(bottom right)
Artist
Robert Neubecker
Title
Childhood Immunization Chart
Client
Joyce Foundation, Chicago

Artist
Ari Plikat
Title
Clown jongliert mit Maüsen
Client
Wustmann & Ziegenfeuter,
TK Production, Dortmund

Artist
Ari Plikat
Title
Goldfisch Dompteur
Client
Wustmann & Ziegenfeuter,
TK Production, Dortmund

Artist
Vikki Liogier
Client
DMB & B for Gordon's Gin

Artist
Stuart Harrison
Title
Cheeky Banter and all out Spiceyness
at the "Crack" Public House,
Liverpool, England
Client
COSH Boys On Public Assistance Ltd.

Artist
Stuart Harrison
Title
Chicago Steroids BUM RUSH The Show
Client
Cheese Hammer Quarterly

Artist
Stuart Harrison
Title
Daytripper:
I'm a Man in Space!!!
Client
Bongo Butt Frenzy

Artist
Nishan Akgulian,
David Goldman Agency
Title
The No Fun League
Client
Sports Illustrated

Artist
Nishan Akgulian,
David Goldman Agency
Title
The Big Punch

Artist
Nishan Akgulian,
David Goldman Agency
Title
Ickey Shuffles for
the Last Time
Client
Sports Illustrated

Artist
Alex Tiani
Title
Implementation
Client
Merisel Inc.

Artist
Alex Tiani
Title
Marketing Department
Client
Source Magazine

(left)
Artist
Maggie LIng
Title
Windows of the Soul
Client
Brown Packaging

(right)
Artist
Alex Tiani
Title
Mood Swings
Client
Self Magazine

Artist
Kevin Faerber
Client
EM-SPACE
(The Princes Trust)

Artist
Bernard Custodio
Title
Catastrophe

(top left & right, bottom left)
Artist
Frederic Morel

(center)
Artist
Roger De Muth
Title
Linhoff the Cat Photographer
Client
Ray Beale Photography

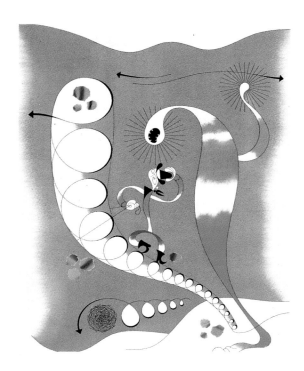

Artist
Anthony Colbert
Client
Publication -
'Resurgence' Magazine

Artist
Anthony Colbert
Client
Publication -
'Resurgence' Magazine

Artist
Lee Calderon
Title
Hallie and Dave

Artist
Lee Calderon
Title
When God
Can't Save the Queen

ANIMALS

◁◁ *Artist*
Karen Johnson,
Garden Studio
Title
I want you

Artist
Braldt Bralds,
c/o Artbank Illustration Library,
London, England
Title
Party Animals

Artist
Nicola Bayley,
c/o Artbank International,
London, England

Artist
Nicola Bayley,
c/o Artbank International,
London, England
Title
Two by Two

Artist
Mario Kessler
Title
Book Title - Illustration
Client
Loewes Verlag

Artist
Philip Bliss
Title
Irena Guinness at "Hutchins Y + R"
Client
Xerox Corporation

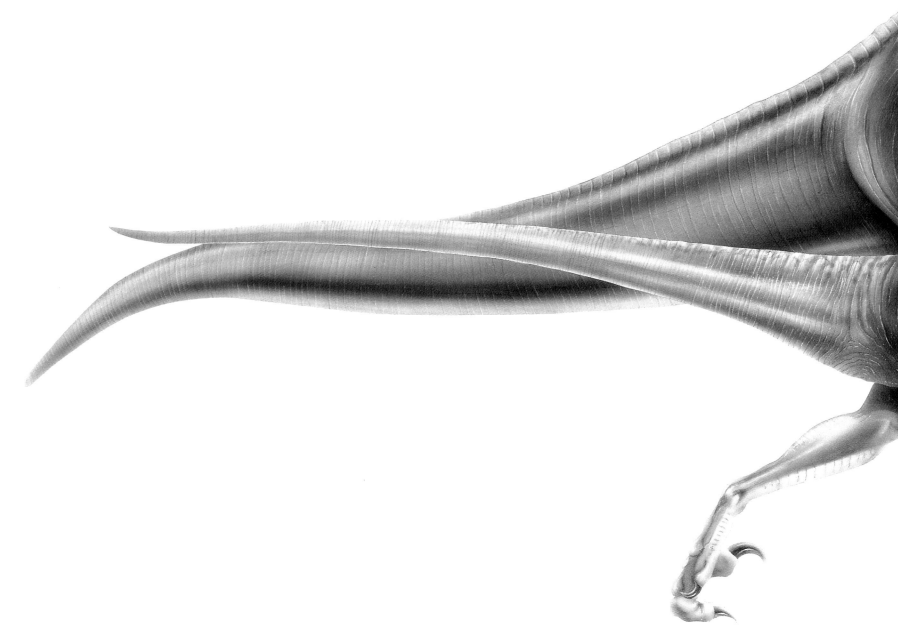

Artist
Terry Pastor
Title
T. Rex + Velociraptor
Client
Orbis, England

Artist
Richard Lewington, Garden Studio
Title
Iguanadon
Client
Readers' Digest Books

▷ *Artist*
Alain BERTRAND
Title
Cheetha
Client
Schering-Labaratory

Artist
Gregory M. Hurley
Title
Ocelot

Artist
Guy Porfirio,
Ceci Bartels Associates

Artist
Leland Klanderman,
Ceci Bartels Associates

Artist
Bill Bruning,
Ceci Bartels Associates

Artist
June Workman
Title
Rising Above

Artist
Cliff Wright
Title
Bear & Kite
Client
Harper Collins

Artist
Ean Taylor,
XING Art Productions GmbH
Title
Horse and Groom

Artist
Glenn Harrington
Title
Rathas Challenge
Client
McMillan Publisher ©1994

Artist
Mario Kessler
Title
Concept and Design of various Biotopes:
"Life at a Dead Track"
Client
Gong Publishing

Artist
Mario Kessler
Title
Concept and Design of various Biotopes:
"Animals and Plants of the Brushwood"
Client
Gong Publishing

Artist
Mario Kessler
Title
Concept and Design of various Biotopes:
"Winter in a Suburban Backyard"
Client
Gong Publishing

Artist
Mario Kessler
Title
Concept and Design of various Biotopes:
"Winter Season in the Woods"
Client
Gong Publishing

Artist
Eric Tenney
Client
Landsdowne Euro, England

Artist
Eric Tenney
Client
Landsdowne Euro, England

Artist
Eric Tenney
Client
J. Sainsbury

(top right)
Artist
Graham Austin,
Garden Studio
Title
Brolly Sir !
Client
Brompton Agency
(St. Bruno Tobacco)

Artist
Germana Conca

◁ *Artist*
Eric Tenney
Client
J. Sainsbury

◁◁ *Artist*
Eric Tenney

Artist
Germana Conca

Artist
Peter Warner
Title
Go-Cat cinnamon tabby cat -
Go-Cat dry catfood packaging design
Client
Nestlé / Design Bridge, London

Artist
Peter Warner
Title
Afghan Hound and Sealpoint Siamese -
from Gaines Peter Warner 1993 Calendar
Client
Ajinomoto General Foods/Tokyu Agency Inc, Tokyo

Artist
Peter Warner
Title
Milka Cow -
Milka Lila Pause Billboard
Client
Suchard Milka /
Young and Rubicam SA, Paris

Artist
Peter Warner
Title
Golden Retriever -
Winalot dogmeal packaging
Client
Dalgety Spillers Foods /
Coley Porter Bell, London

Artist
Peter Warner
Title
Sand Cat (Felis margarita) in
North African desert habitat

Artist
Peter Warner
Title
Common Buzzard and Rabbit Prey -
Illustration from "Atlas of Animal Migration"
by Cathy Jarman
Client
Aldus Books, London

Artist
Peter Warner
Title
Hush Puppies Dog -
Logo design for vehicle livery and billboards
Client
British Shoe Corporation /
Newton and Godin, London

Artist
Julian Willis,
Tree Top Studio
Title
The Alpage

(top left)
Artist
Peter Warner
Title
Piglet - Childrens' Book Jacket
Client
Hodder & Stoughton, London

(bottom left)
Artist
Gioia Marchegiani
Title
Picture of a Cat

(top right)
Artist
Peter Warner
Title
Badger Cub - Childrens'
Book Jacket
Client
Hodder & Stoughton, London

(bottom right)
Artist
Germana Conca

Artist
Bruce Garrity
Title
Bulldog

Artist
Ben Lustenhouwer,
The Artbox bv

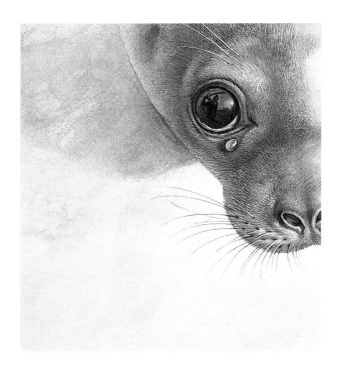

Artist
Peter Warner
Title
"Water" - an Interpretation for
a Conservation Diary
Client
Hilary Bradford Associates, Milan

(top right)
Artist
Victor Vaccaro
Title
Jungle Animals

Artist
Mario Kessler
Title
Animal Portraits for
a Television Series
Client
German TV

Artist
Mario Kessler
Title
Animal Portraits for
a Television Series
Client
German TV

Artist
Gabriella Giandelli
Title
Gatto Con Glistivali
Client
Dolce Vita - Italia Magazine

Artist
Jan Machalek

Title
Series of the Illustrations for Book
"Animal Stories"
Client
Key Porter Books Ltd., Toronto

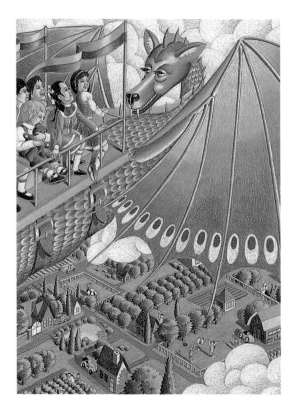

Artist
Jan Machalek

Title
Series of the Illustrations for Book
"Animal Stories"
Client
Key Porter Books Ltd., Toronto

Artist
Lilla Rogers
Title
Cat Kitty Cat
Client
Gulliver Publishing Ltd.,
Japan

Artist
Lilla Rogers
Title
Meow Cat
Client
Gulliver Publishing Ltd.,
Japan

Artist
Ari Plikat

Artist
Ari Plikat

cat kitty cat

meow

cat

Artist
Hirotaka Hayashi
Title
We Love the Earth

Artist
Michelangelo Rossino,
A.I. Member
Title
Vincent Van Duck
Client
Canard

◁◁ *Artist*
Robert Giusti,
c/o Artbank International,
London, England

Artist
Raphael Montoliu,
Ceci Bartels Associates

Artist
John Fox, Arcana

Artist
Mario Kessler
Title
Concept and Design of various Biotopes:
"Winter Season under Water"
Client
Gong Publishing

Artist
Mario Kessler
Title
Concept and Design of various Biotopes:
"Life in the Mountain Creek"
Client
Gong Publishing

Artist
Giuseppe Cafagna

Artist
Mike Atkinson,
Garden Studio
Title
Pee Wit
Client
Fine Art Print

▷ Artist
Thomas Cain
Title
Save the Rainforest
Client
Supply America, Inc.

Artist
Thomas Cain
Title
Fish of the Sea
Client
Supply America, Inc.

Artist
Giuseppe Cafagna
Title
Hoazin

Artist
© Linda Montgomery
Artist Rep : Irmeli Holmberg
Client
Pierre Belvedere Inc.

Artist
June Workman
Title
Booger

Artist
Guy Porfirio,
Ceci Bartels Associates

Artist
Monica Di Folco
Title
South American Frog

Artist
Justin Carroll,
Ceci Bartels Associates

Artist
Catherine Diez-Luckie
Title
A Frog asks "How?"
Client
Rockport Publishers

Artist
Peter Bartczak,
Clownbank Studio
Title
Painting Pelican
Client
Pelikan Inks

Artist
Peter Bartczak,
Clownbank Studio
Title
Punk Parrot
Client
Paper Moon Graphics

Artist
Michelangelo Rossino,
A.I. Member
Title
Duck Velasquez
Client
Canard

Artist
Bill Wood
Title
Green Turtle
(Christmas Island)
Client
Australia Post

(bottom left)
Artist
Paolo D'Altan,
A.I. Member
Title
Oops !
Client
Algida Icecream

(bottom right)
Artist
Paolo D'Altan,
A.I. Member
Client
Baldoni & Dal Borgo

Artist
Bill Wood
Title
Red Crab
(Christmas Island)
Client
Australia Post

(bottom left)
Artist
Paolo D'Altan,
A.I. Member
Client
Baldoni & Dal Borgo

(bottom right)
Artist
Paolo D'Altan,
A.I. Member
Client
Baldoni & Dal Borgo

Artist
Robert Giusti,
c/o Artbank International,
London, England

Artist
Paolo D'Altan,
A.I. Member
Title
Bufo-Bufo
Client
Codacon

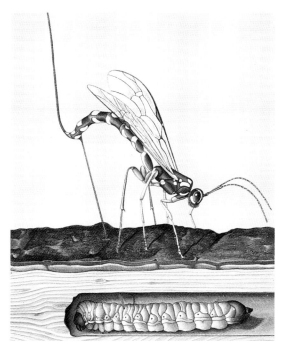

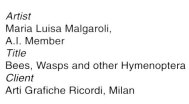

Artist
Maria Luisa Malgaroli,
A.I. Member
Title
Bees, Wasps and other Hymenoptera
Client
Arti Grafiche Ricordi, Milan

(top right)
Artist
Mario Kessler
Title
A Praying Mantis catches
a Grasshopper

Artist
Mario Kessler
Title
Animal Portraits for a
Televison Series
Client
German TV

Artist
Mario Kessler
Title
Illustration for Nature Encyclopedia
of Europe
Client
Bertelsmann Publishing

Artist
Mario Kessler
Title
Animal Portraits for a
Television Series
Client
German TV

Artist
Daniela Cicchetti,
A.I. Member
Title
Maggiolino nel sottobosco

Artist
Roberta Primerano,
A.I. Member
Title
Butterflies

Artist
Edith Buenen,
The Artbox bv

Artist
David Scanlan
Title
Giant Kelp
Client
San Diego Union-Tribune

Artist
Hirotaka Hayashi
Title
Clean Ocean

Artist
Pippa Sterne
Title
Heading up stream
Client
Morris Nicholson Cartwright

Artist
Maria Letizia Cariello,
A.I. Member

Artist
Maria Letizia Cariello,
A.I. Member

Artist
Vicky Lowe
Title
Penguins, Regents Park

Artist
Vicky Lowe
Title
Penn Ponds
Client
John Menzies

Artist
Shirley Barker
Title
The English Oak
Client
Good-Housekeeping Magazine

Artist
Marie Lessard
Title
For The Outspoken
Client
Henri Vezina -
A Men's Clothing Store

Artist
Shirley Barker
Title
The Symbolic Fish
Client
Taste Magazine

Artist
Marie Lessard
Title
For The Outstanding
Client
Henri Vezina -
A Men's Clothing Store

Artist
Phillip Tyler

Artist
Ben Campbell,
c/o Artbank International,
London, England

Artist
Melvyn Grant,
c/o Artbank Illustration Library,
London, England

Artist
Lindy Burnett,
Ceci Bartels Associates

Artist
Abe Gurvin
Title
The True Value of Wholesome Food
Client
Health Associates

Artist
Andrew Riley,
Garden Studio
Title
Bread and Rolls

Artist
Michael Fisher,
Garden Studio
Title
Tasty Steak
Client
Lowe Howard Spink (Tesco)

◁ *Artist*
Ben Verkaaik,
The Artbox bv
Client
Dutch Cheese Board

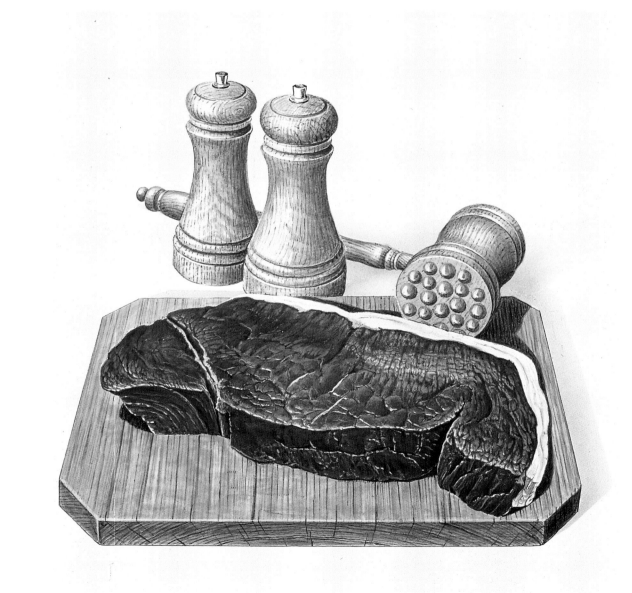

Artist
Andy Zito
Title
Food and Wine of Spain - Map
Client
Agricultural Board of Spain

Artist
Carme Julià
Title
Summer Still-Life
Client
Guarro Casas

Artist
Lucille Prache (Klaxon),
[DE-VI-ZU] Images Publiques,
Paris

(top left)
Artist
Guy Porfirio,
Ceci Bartels Associates

(bottom left)
Artist
Abe Gurvin
Title
Mexican Treat
Client
Casa de España

(top right)
Artist
Joanna Roy
Title
Vegetable Lasagna
Client
Country Journal Magazine

(bottom right)
Artist
Ivor Coburn,
Garden Studio
Title
Haute Cuisine
Client
Fine Art (Oils)

Artist
Katherine Salentine
Agent: Janice Stefanski
Title
Apple & Grapes
Client
Poster

Artist
Katherine Salentine
Agent: Janice Stefanski
Title
Mantel Piece

Artist
Abe Gurvin
Title
Orange
Client
Sunkist Growers,
Foote-Cone-Belding

Artist
Charles Waller
Title
For My Teacher
Client
Book Jacket -
Peter Pauper Press

Artist
Klaus Winckler
Title
Poster for Baby Food
Client
Milupa

Artist
Michael Ogden
Title
Olvarit Baby Foods
Client
Alliance, Bristol, UK

Artist
Bill Mundy,
Garden Studio
Title
Fruit of the Vine
Client
Lowe Howard Spink (Tesco)

Artist
Eric Robson,
Garden Studio
Title
Harvest Festival
Client
BMP

Artist
Celia Chester

Artist
Celia Chester
Title
Raspberries

Artist
Alessandra Gazzoni,
A.I. Member
Title
Pelati Cirio

Artist
Abe Gurvin
Title
Mexican Food
Client
Tyson Foods

Artist
Guy Porfirio,
Ceci Bartels Associates

Artist
Di Dio Giuseppe

Artist
Bud Smallwood
Title
Ice Cream
Client
Praxair Newsletter,
Huebner Design

Artist
Colin Brown
Title
Golden Syrup Cake

Artist
Kim Lane
Title
SPA Canned Drinks
Client
Michael Peters Associates

Artist
Mike Moran
Title
Dig in Winter for Summer Crops

SCIENCE FICTION

Artist
Darrel Anderson / Braid
Title
Particle Giant
Client
Penwell Publishing

◁ *Artist*
Wayne Watford,
Ceci Bartels Associates
Title
Robocop

◁◁ *Artist*
Rick Berry / Braid
Title
Dirty Work (Book Cover)
Client
Ziesing Publisher

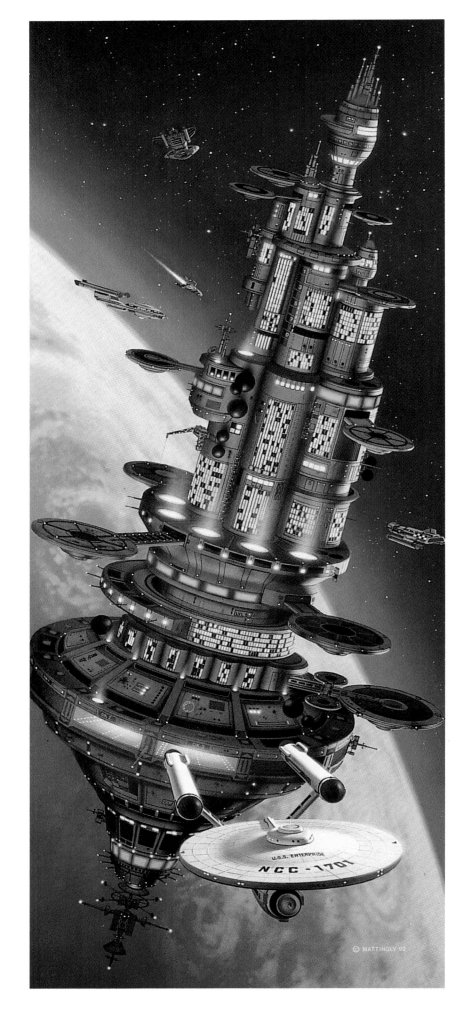

Artist
Darrel Anderson / Braid
Title
Crusin' 1993 Digital

(left)
Artist
David B. Mattingly
Title
Star Trek : Log 4
Client
Del Rey Books

(right)
Artist
David B. Mattingly
Title
Star Trek : Log 6
Client
Del Rey Books

Artist
David B. Mattingly
Title
Saint Joan and the Computer
Client
Amazing Stories

Artist
David B. Mattingly
Title
The Subway Wizard
Client
Amazing Stories

Artist
Simon Williams,
Garden Studio
Title
Space Wars
Client
Video Cover

Artist
Steinar Lund,
Garden Studio
Title
Science of the Future
Client
Video Cover

Artist ▷
Chris Moore,
c/o Artbank Illustration Library,
London, England

Artist
Bernard Gudynas,
Zap Art
Title
Mozart for Philips

Artist
Chris Spollen,
Moonlight Press Studio
© Chris Spollen 1995
Title
Radio Robots
Client
Moonlight Prints

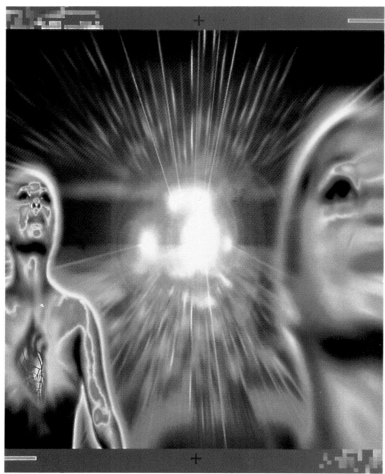
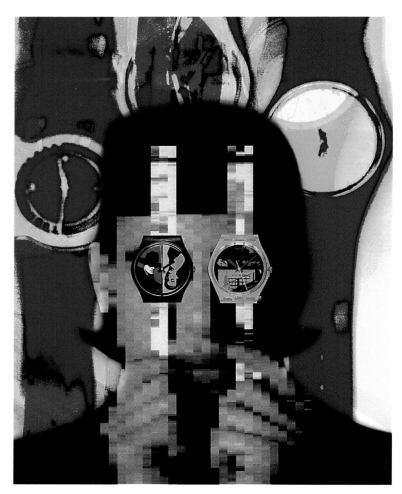

Artist
Peter Roseler
Title
Captain Future
Client
Edition of Pharmacie/
Magazine Editorial

Artist
Bernard Gudynas,
Zap Art
Title
Into the Interface
Client
The Design Council

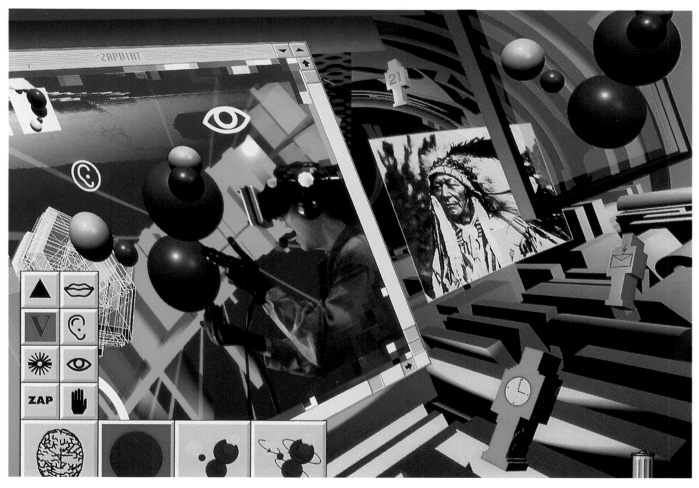

(top left)
Artist
Peter Gudynas
Title
Snowcrash

(bottom left)
Artist
Peter Gudynas
Title
Unmanned Futures

(top right)
Artist
Peter Gudynas
Title
Global Head

(bottom right)
Artist
Bernard Gudynas,
Zap Art
Title
Swatch Consumer

Artist
Patricia McShane / M.A.D.
Title
Spread Illustration
Client
Raygun Magazine

Artist
Victor Stabin
Title
RCA Mural
Client
RCA/BMG Corporate Headquarters NYC

Artist
Andy Zito
Title
Aries Astrology Image
Client
The Image Bank

(top right)
Artist
Andy Zito
Title
Leo Astrology Image
Client
The Image Bank

Artist
Erik Adigard / M.A.D.
Title
Images and Tools Lecture
Client
Macworld 92, I & T Lecture

Artist
Frank Langford

Artist
Frank Langford

Artist
Max Ellis
Title
Traffic Wardens - Birds of Prey

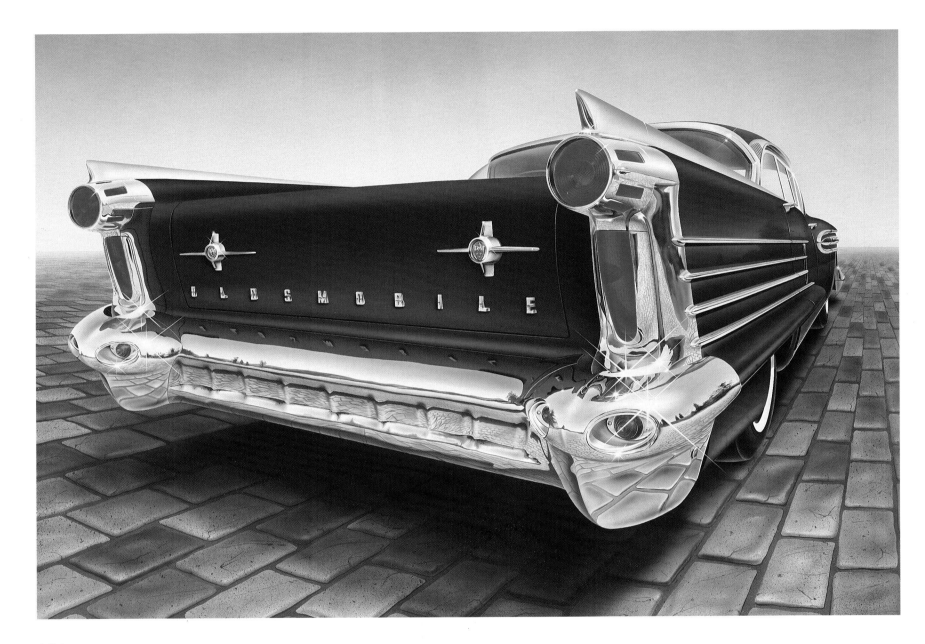

Artist
Colin Brown
Title
Oldsmobile

◁◁ *Artist*
Cathy Doutreligne,
[DE-VI-ZU] Images Publiques,
Paris

Artist
Guerrino Boatto,
A.I. Member
Title
FORD Calendar '93
Client
FORD Europe

Artist
Guerrino Boatto,
A.I. Member
Title
FORD Calendar '93
Client
FORD Europe

Artist
Guerrino Boatto,
A.I. Member
Client
Pioneer Audio Car

Artist
Guerrino Boatto,
A.I. Member

Artist
Guerrino Boatto,
A.I. Member
Title
FORD Calendar '93
Client
FORD Europe

Artist ▷
Pim Sekeris,
The Artbox bv

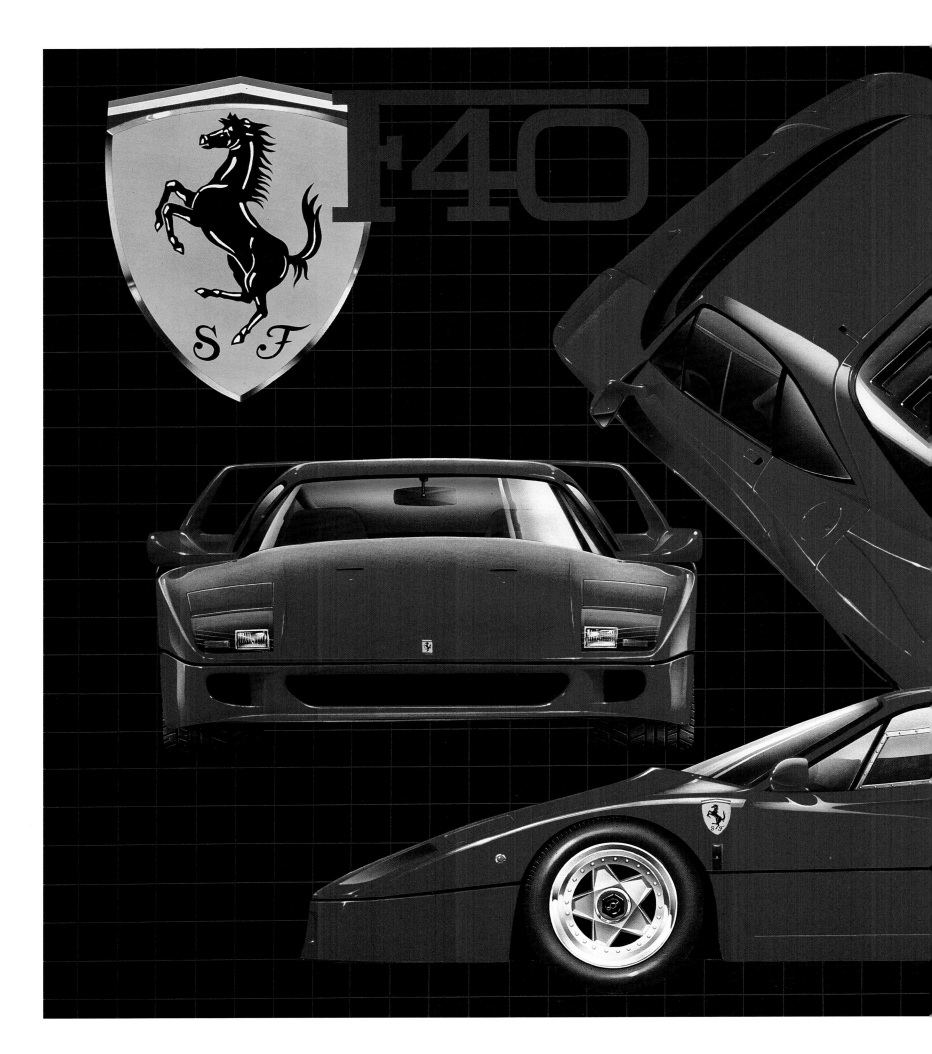

Artist
Michael Hasted,
XING Art Productions GmbH
Title
Todeslinie - Short Story
Client
Freundin Magazine, Munich

Artist
Terry Pastor
Title
Ferrari F40
Client
B.M.P. England

Artist
Kevin Newman,
Ceci Bartels Associates

(top right)
Artist
Wayne Watford,
Ceci Bartels Associates

Artist
Harold Cleworth,
c/o Artbank International,
London, England
Title
1955 Mercedes Gullwing

Artist
Harold Cleworth,
c/o Artbank International,
London, England
Title
1933 Packard

Artist
Wayne Watford,
Ceci Bartels Associates
Client
R. J. Reynolds

Artist
Bernie Walsh
Title
Advanced Sports Coupe

Artist
Bernie Walsh
Title
Serena
Client
Nissan, Australia

Artist
Bernie Walsh
Title
Nissan GTR
Client
Nissan, Australia

Artist
Bernie Walsh
Title
Nissan Patrol
Client
Nissan, Australia

Artist
Wayne Watford,
Ceci Bartels Associates
Client
R. J. Reynolds

Artist
Arthur Phillips
Title
Motor-Cycle Cutway

Artist
Alain BERTRAND
Title
Chroma
Client
FIAT, France

Artist
Lonnie Busch

Artist
Andy Zito
Title
European Bullet Train
Client
Pacific Bell Telephone

Artist
Alain BERTRAND
Title
TGV Highspeed Train
Client
S.N.C.F.

Artist
George F. Heiron,
c/o Artbank International,
London, England
Title
The Great Days

Artist
Martin Woodward
Title
Brede Class Lifeboat

Artist
Michael Hasted,
XING Art Productions GmbH
Title
The Blue Train
Client
Playboy Magazine, Munich

Artist
Michael Ogden
Title
Ship for P & O Cruises
Client
Still Price Lintas, London

Artist
Ernest Nisbet,
Garden Studio
Title
Flight over England
Client
Print Edition

Artist
Colin Brown
Title
AST Plane
Client
British Aerospace

Artist
Lynn Chadwick,
Garden Studio
Title
Cottage Gardens
Client
Sunday Times

Artist
Michael Fisher,
Garden Studio
Title
Buildings Today
Client
ICI

◁◁ *Artist*
Colin Brown
Title
Tower Block
Client
Galileo Software

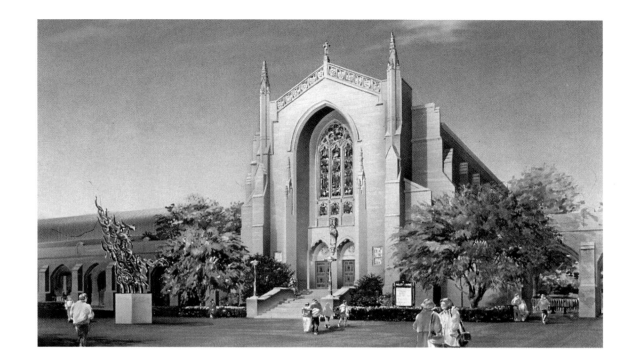

Artist
Anita S. Bice
Title
Marsh Chapel, Boston University
Client
New Horizons, Ltd.

Artist
Anita S. Bice
Title
The Quad, Harvard Medical School
Client
New Horizons, Ltd.

Artist
Bud Smallwood
Title
The Cyclone
Client
Computer Artist Magazine

Artist
Bud Smallwood
Title
Wonderland

Artist
Peter Edgeley
Title
Retail & Tower Complex,
Shanghai, China
Client
Nick Bochsler,
Bochsler & Partners,
Architects, Melbourne

Artist
Bud Smallwood
Title
Chicago, It's Awesome
Client
Mitsubishi Press Demo

Artist
Pim Sekeris,
The Artbox bv

Artist
Pim Sekeris,
The Artbox bv

Artist
Bernie Walsh
Title
Sydney Opera House

Artist
Peter Edgeley
Title
Singapore Waterfront
Client
Keith Griffiths, Griffiths Associates,
Architects, Hong Kong

Artist
Andy Zito
Title
Dollar Sign Staircase
Client
The Image Bank

Artist
Stephen Conlin

Artist
Peter Edgeley
Title
Shopping Mall, Melbourne
Client
Dale Sprankle,
Sprankle Lynd & Sprague Architects
San Francisco

Artist
Peter Edgeley
Title
Pacific Plaza Atrium, Hong Kong
Client
Keith Griffiths,
Griffiths Associates
Architects, Hong Kong

Artist ▷
Dolf Stekhoven bNO
Client
Netherlands Railroad Company

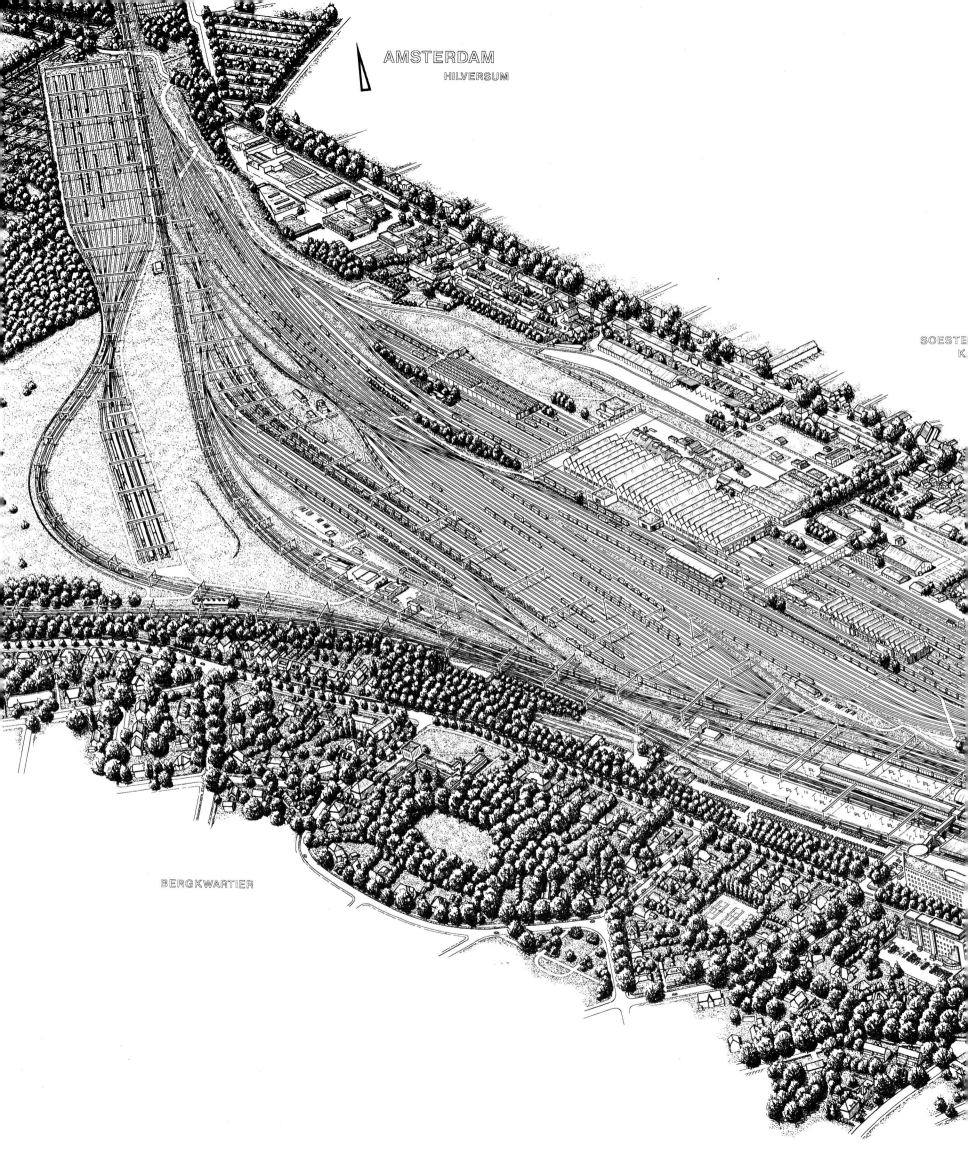

AMSTERDAM
HILVERSUM

SOESTE
K.

BERGKWARTIER

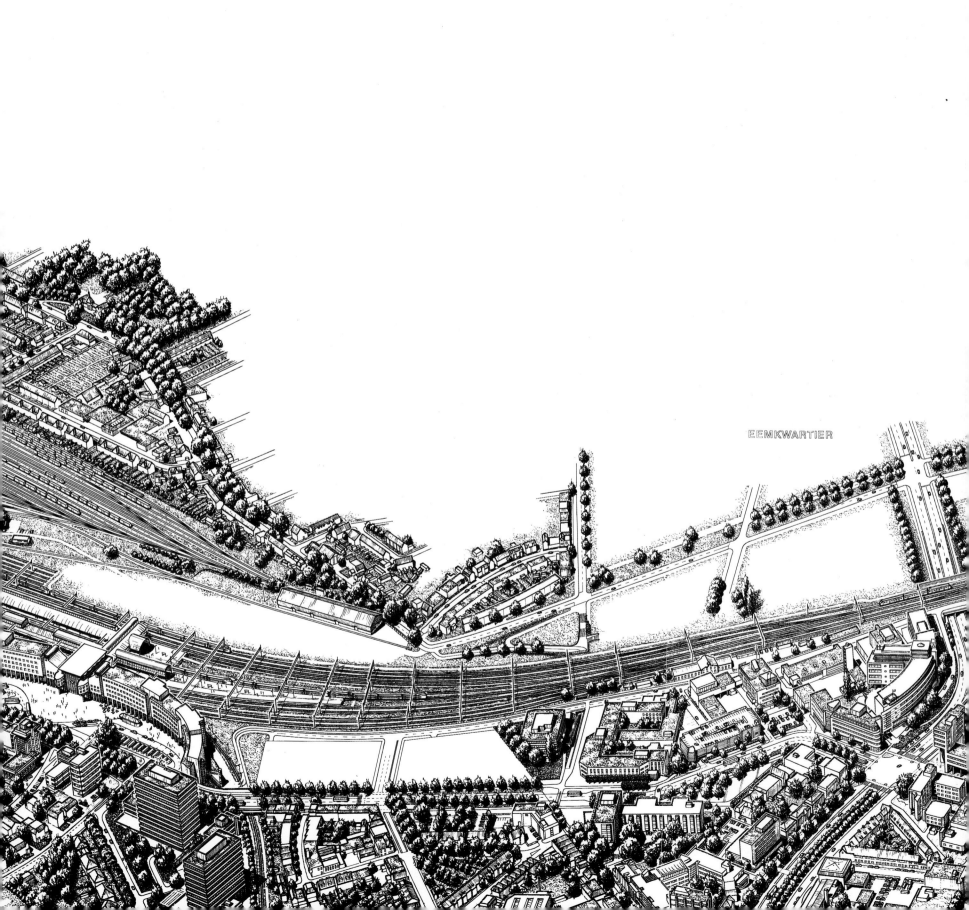

EEMKWARTIER

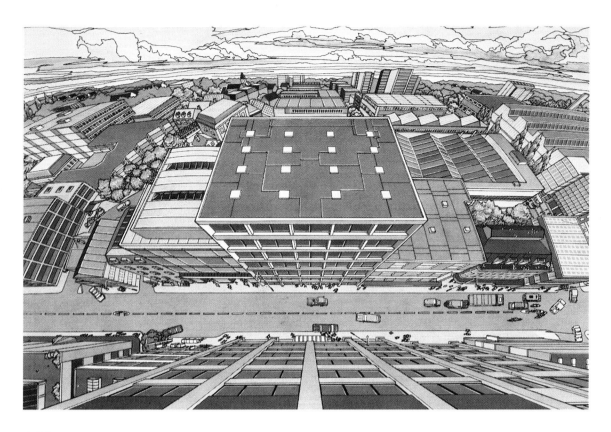

Artist
Thierry Clauson
Title
La Tour
Client
Travail Personnel

Artist
Michael Fisher,
Garden Studio
Title
Where to go (Vertigo!)
Client
Tarmac

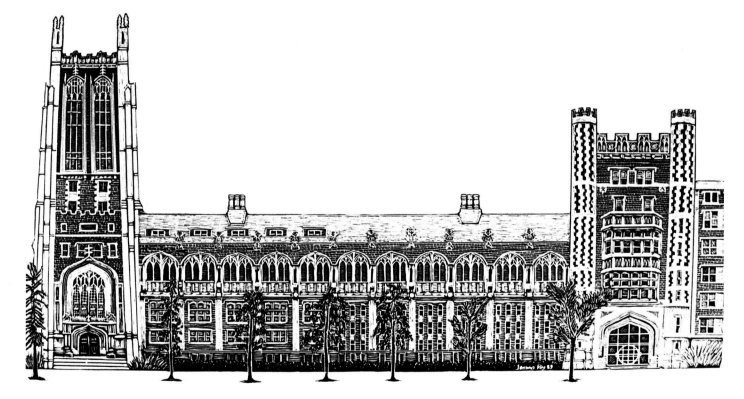

Artist
Joanna Roy
Title
Union Theological Seminary
Client
Union Theological Seminary

Artist
Paul Rogers
Title
City Panorama
Client
Panasonic Electronics

Artist
Luiz Yudo,
The Artbox bv

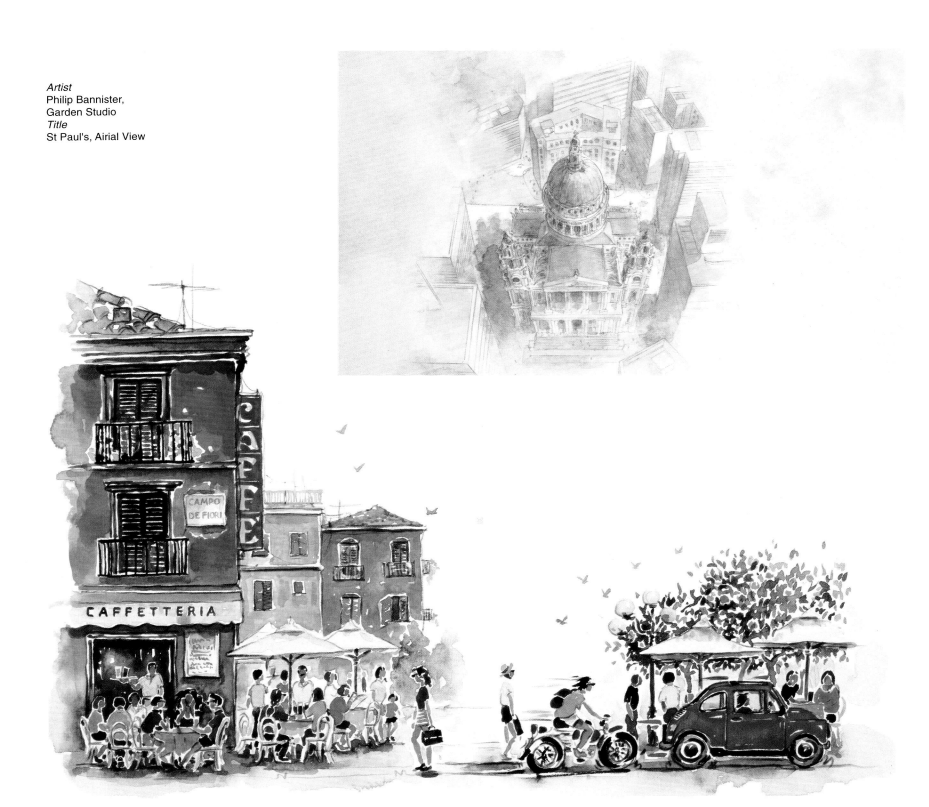

Artist
Philip Bannister,
Garden Studio
Title
St Paul's, Airial View

Artist
Vicky Lowe
Title
Piazza, Verona
Client
Kingfisher Books

Artist
Paolo Rui, A.I. Member
Title
Once Upon a Duomo ...
Client
Fotolito Fram

Artist
Raphael Montoliu,
Ceci Bartels Associates

Artist
Ingo Fast
Title
A Hospital at Work
Client
© 1995, Steck-Vaughn Company

Artist
Liz Roberts
Title
Tiled Roof, Portofino

Artist
Ingo Fast
Title
A Hospital at Work
Client
© 1995, Steck-Vaughn Company

Artist
Victoria Kann
Title
House for Sale
Client
Louisville Magazine

Artist
Shirley Barker
Title
The Michelin Building
Client
Conran Design

Artist
Vicky Lowe
Title
Clock Shop, Auxere

Artist
Raphael Montoliu,
Ceci Bartels Associates

Artist
Alan Mazzetti
Title
Flight

Artist
Alan Mazzetti
Title
Rise & Fall

◁◁ *Artist*
Alan Mazzetti
Title
Home

Artist
Rosemary Woods
Client
Hodder & Stoughton

Artist
Rosemary Woods
Client
Poolbeg Press

Artist
Lucile Prache (Klaxon),
[DE-VI-ZU] Images Publiques,
Paris

(bottom left)
Artist
Cathy Doutreligne,
[DE-VI-ZU] Images Publiques,
Paris

(bottom right)
Artist
Cathy Doutreligne,
[DE-VI-ZU] Images Publiques,
Paris

Artist
Lucile Prache (Klaxon),
[DE-VI-ZU] Images Publiques,
Paris

(bottom left)
Artist
Cathy Doutreligne,
[DE-VI-ZU] Images Publiques,
Paris

(bottom right)
Artist
Cathy Doutreligne,
[DE-VI-ZU] Images Publiques,
Paris

(opposite & top)
Artist
Cathy Doutreligne,
[DE-VI-ZU] Images Publiques,
Paris

Artist
Gabriella Giandelli
Title
Stanza
Client
Esquire - Italia Magazine

(top right)
Artist
Paolo D'Altan,
A.I. Member
Title
Tribute to Gary Kelley
Client
Cotton Color

Artist
Lucile Prache (Klaxon),
[DE-VI-ZU] Images Publiques,
Paris
Client
FNAC, France

Artist
Stefano Ricci
Title
Hands Off Cain

Artist
Lucile Prache (Klaxon),
[DE-VI-ZU] Images Publiques,
Paris

Artist
Ted Wright,
Ceci Bartels Associates

Artist
Dick Prins,
The Artbox bv

Artist
Fred Otnes

Artist
Fred Otnes

Artist
Marie Lessard
Title
Piazza Navona
Client
The New York Times

Artist
Melinda Beck
Title
Window Pain
Client
Purgatory Pie Press

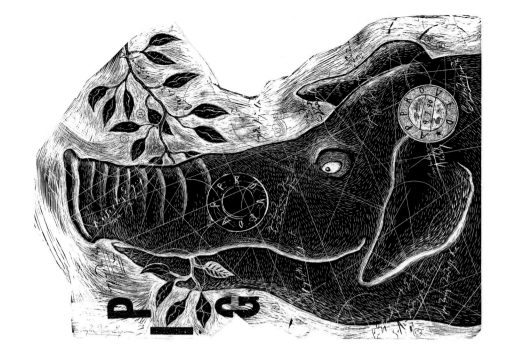

Artist
Joanna Roy
Title
Let there be Light for Indoor Plants
Client
The New York Times

(top left)
Artist
Walter Van Lotringen,
The Artbox bv

Artist
Stefano Ricci
Title
Mardi 18 Novembre 1947
Client
Il Navile. Edizioni Grafiche

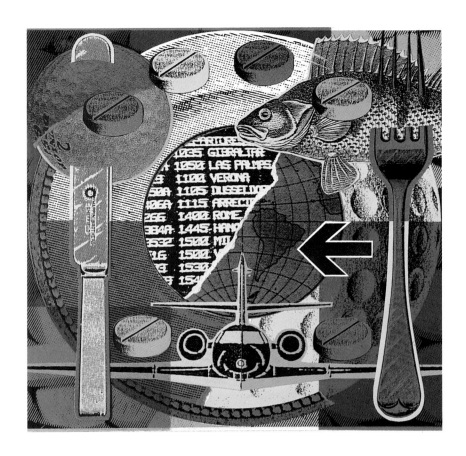

Artist
Dettmer E.Otto
Title
Problems in Establishing
a Legal System in
Eastern European Countries
Client
Harrington Kilbride,
London

Artist
Dettmer E. Otto
Title
Stress in Work and
Home Environments
Client
Training Information
Network, Middlesex,
Britain

(top left)
Artist
Paul Bateman
Title
Gifts for Doctors from
Pharmaceutical Companies
Client
Haymarket Publishing -
General Practitioner Magazine

(bottom left)
Artist
Paul Bateman
Title
Staggering Stories of Ferdinand de Bargos
Client
BBC Enterprises, Radio Times Magazine

(top right)
Artist
Paul Bateman
Title
Censorship
Client
New Statesman & Society and
Channel 4 Television

(bottom right)
Artist
Dettmer E. Otto
Title
Phasing out CFCs
Client
International Thompson Business Publishing

Artist
Rick Sealock
Title
Ranch for Women
Client
Detroit Free Press

Artist
Rick Sealock
Title
Mission Possible!
Client
American Medical News

Artist
Rick Sealock
Title
Brochure Cover for
Highwood Music Festival
Client
Highwood Music Festival

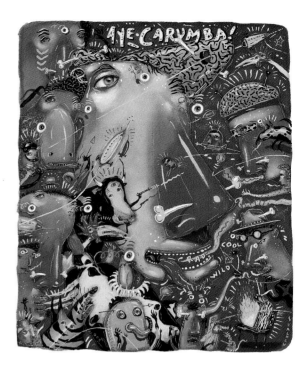

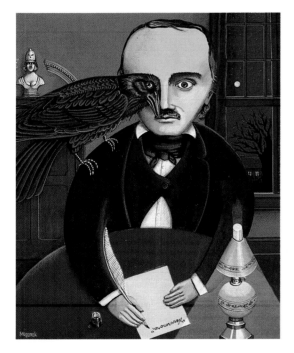

Artist
Rick Sealock
Title
Master Disaster
Client
American Medical News

Artist
Robert Meganck,
Communication Design Inc.
Title
Poe
Client
Running Press Book Publishers

Artist
Rick Sealock
Title
Weekend with the Reaper
Client
Forum Magazine

Artist
Joshua Gosfield
Title
1914

Artist
Rick Sealock
Title
Advertising Illustration
to sell Video Games
Client
Sears USA

Artist
Joshua Gosfield
Title
Diana Vreeland
Client
New Yorker

Artist
Jordin Isip
Title
Nightclubs
Client
South Beach Magazine

Artist
Jordin Isip
Title
Valentines
Client
City Paper

Artist
Jordin Isip
Title
Scanscape
Client
Mondo 2000

Artist
Jordin Isip
Title
In Living Color
Client
Rolling Stone

Artist
John R Nelson,
Ceci Bartels Associates

Artist
Erik Adigard / M.A.D.
Title
Future Fashion
Client
VOGUE Magazine

Artist
Dan Yaccarino
Title
Tandem Riders
Client
Troika Magazine

Artist
Dan Yaccarino
Title
Man and Machine

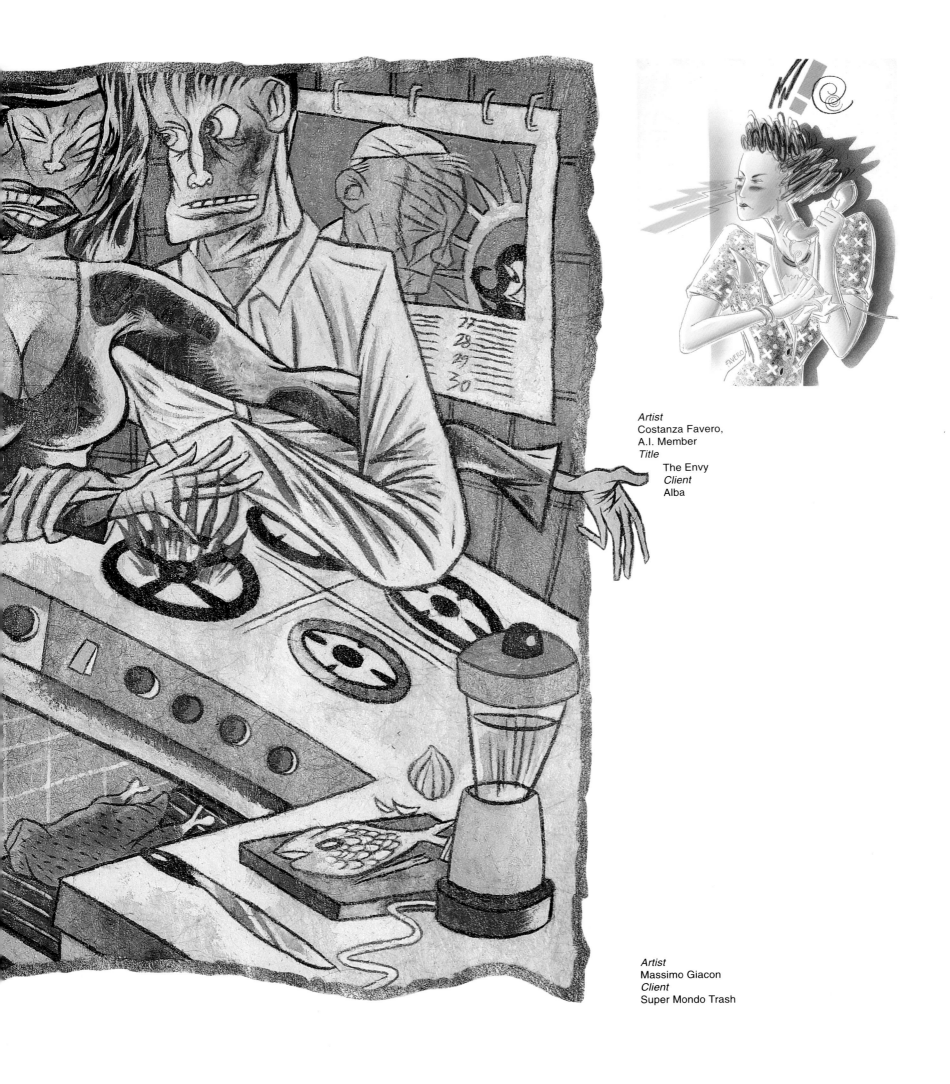

Artist
Costanza Favero,
A.I. Member
Title
    The Envy
Client
Alba

Artist
Massimo Giacon
Client
Super Mondo Trash

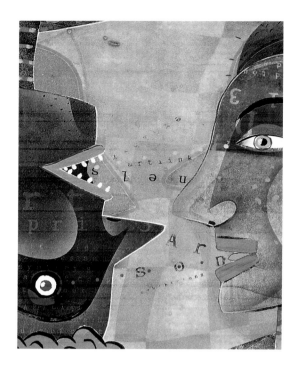

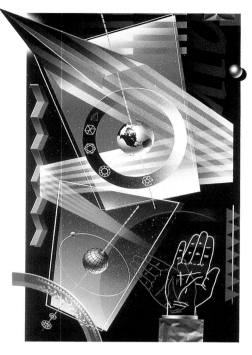

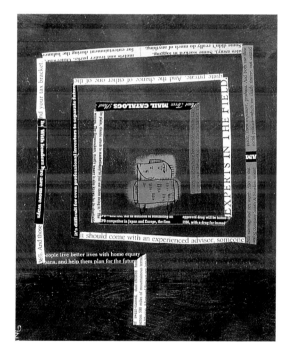

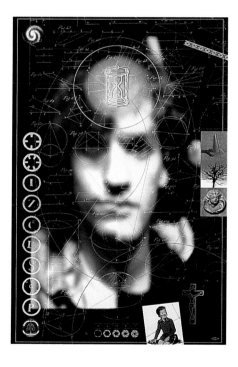

Artist
John R. Nelson,
Ceci Bartels Associates

Artist
James Yang,
David Goldman Agency
Title
Text Borders
Client
WordPerfect Magazine

Artist
Louis Fishauf / Reactor
Title
Future Vision
Client
Macworld Expositions

Artist
Roy Wiemann
Title
Office Outlook
Client
Miller Freeman Publications

Artist
Roy Wiemann
Title
Airplane
Client
Clare Jett & Associates

Artist
Louis Fishauf / Reactor
Title
REM / Out of Time
Client
Rolling Stone Magazine

Artist
Tim Clark
Title
Day Shift
Client
Virgin Records

Artist
Christopher Palmer
Title
Artists' Nightmare

Artist
Louis Fishauf / Reactor
Title
Quality is King!
Client
Eric Baker Design

Artist
Lesley Saddington
Title
Dancing Around the Sun

(top left)
Artist
David Wink
Title
Lockeroom Lookout
Client
The Atlanta Journal/Constitution

(bottom left)
Artist
Vikki Liogier
Title
Star Watch
Client
Options Magazine, U.K.

(top right)
Artist
Mark T. Smith
Title
That Damn Dog

(bottom right)
Artist
David Wink
Title
Rites of Passage
Client
David Wink Inc.

Artist
Davide Bressan
Title
Cassaforte
Client
Cassa Di Risparmio Di Parma

Artist ▷▷
Luiz Yudo,
The Artbox bv

Artist
Ned Culic
Title
Master's Apprentices - Electronics
Client
Gas & Fuel, Victoria

Artist
Ned Culic
Title
Master's Apprentices - Painting
Client
Gas & Fuel, Victoria

(top left)
Artist
Tim Davies
Title
The Leisure Process Mural (details of)
"The Blue Note"
Client
The Leisure Process Design Co.

(top right)
Artist
Tim Davies
Title
The Leisure Process Mural
(details of) "Formentera"
Client
The Leisure Process Design Co.

Artist
Vikki Liogier
Title
The Round
Client
South Thames College

Artist
Maria Korusiewicz
Agent: Janice Stefanski
Title
Fresk IV Unicorn

Artist
Albert Pepermans,
[DE-VI-ZU] Images Publiques,
Paris

Artist
Philip Schulz
Title
Couple with Wine

Artist
Buz Walker Teach
Title
Casa Grande Still Life
Client
Luna's Mexican Cafe

Artist
Philip Schulz
Title
High Tea with Pink Crockery

Artist
© Linda Montgomery
Rep : Irmeli Holmberg
Title
Summer
Client
Shopping Bag

Artist
© Kat Thacker
Rep : Irmeli Holmberg
Title
"Brunhilde"
Client
The Metropolitan Opera

Artist
Anja Olschewski
Title
Plantastische Mondfahrt

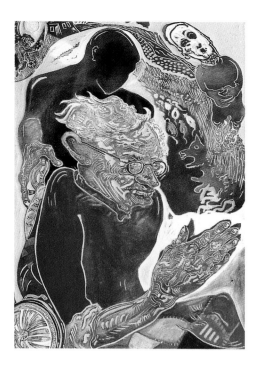

Artist
© Ingo Fast
Title
Democratic Authoritorianism and
State Building in India and Pakistan

Artist
© Ingo Fast
Title
The Greening of Urban Transport

Artist
Philip H. Campbell
Title
Watching Our Garden Grow

Artist
© Ingo Fast
Title
Commuter Transit

Artist
Mario Minichiello
Title
"Going Home" for the Book -
"On the Black Hill" by Bruce Chatwin
Client
Readers' Digest

Artist
Philip H. Campbell
Title
The Drinker

Artist
Mike Knepper
Title
Foreign Legion Still Life
Client
Playboy Magazine

Artist
Mike Knepper
Title
Red Indian Impressions

Artist
Edith Buenen,
The Artbox bv

(top left)
Artist
Mark Surridge
Title
Agricultural Book Fair
Client
The British Council

(bottom left)
Artist
Davide Bressan
Title
Green Monster
Client
Work Inedit

(top right)
Artist
Nuccio Squillaci
Title
Nuppi's Mother

(bottom right)
Artist
Melinda Beck
Title
Where The Wild Things Are

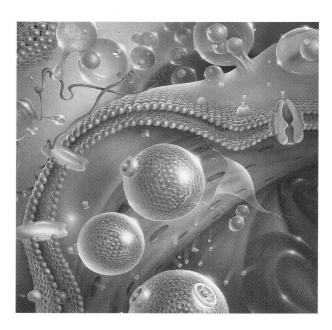

Artist
Keith Kasnot,
Ceci Bartels Associates

(top right)
Artist
Keith Kasnot,
Ceci Bartels Associates

Artist
Thierry Clauson
Title
Univers Organique
Client
Travail Personnel

Artist
Alain BERTRAND
Title
Junkyard
Client
Richard Gangloff

Artist Index

Adam, Lisa
40 Harrisons Street, No 29 F,
NY 10013, USA
Tel : (212) 385-8189
Fax : (212) 385-9630

Anderson, Darrel
1420 Territory Trail, Colorado Springs,
CO 80919, USA
Tel : (719) 535-0407

Anderson, Phillip
HC 35, Box 1022, Route 131 Wiley's Corner,
St. George, Maine 04857, USA
Tel / Fax : (207) 372-6242

Angle, Scott
21051 Barbados Circle,
Huntington Beach, CA 92646, USA
Tel / Fax : (714) 960-8485

Arion, Katherine
1162 N. Orange Grove #6
West Hollywood, CA 90046, USA
Tel : (213) 654-6252

Artbank International
Artist Rep : Rick Goodale
8 Woodcroft Avenue, London NW7 2AG, England
Tel : (181) 906-2288
Fax : (181) 906-2289

The Artbox bv
Artist Rep : Kees Thijssen
Kruislaan 182 - 1098 SK Amsterdam,
The Netherlands
Tel : (20) 668-1551
Fax : (20) 693-9907

Associazione Illustratori (A.I.)
Rep: Paolo D'Altan / Paolo Rui
Via Comelico, 13-20135 Milano, Italy
Tel / Fax : (2) 545-3420

Bag, Mario
Rua Conde De Bonfim, 239/404 Tijuca,
20520-051 Rio de Janeiro, Brazil
Tel / Fax : (21) 228-3604

Barker, Shirley
Flat 4, 83 - 85 Prince of Wales Road,
Kentish Town, London NW5 3LY, England
Tel : (171) 734-7991
Fax : (171) 485-3457

Bartczak, Peter
P O Box 7709, Santa Cruz,
CA 95060, USA
Tel : (408) 426-4247
Fax : (408) 426-8983

Bateman, Paul
18 Chichester House,
Coates Road, Exeter EX2 5RP, England
Tel / Fax : (1392) 435-513

Bates, Leslie
3124 Nassau Road, Oceanside,
NY 11572, USA
Tel : (516) 764-5258

Beck, Melinda
44 Fourth Pl. No. 2 Brooklyn,
NY 11231, USA
Tel : (718) 624-6538
Fax : (718) 624-1994

Bellotto, Sergio
Via Alla Chiesa, 5-21025 Comerio,
Varese, Italy
Tel : (2) 737-635

Berry, Rick
93 Warren St., Arlington, MA 02174, USA
Tel : (617) 648-6375
Fax : (617) 721-5418

Bertrand, Alain
1 Parc Des Fontenelles,
Batimenta - 78870 Bailly, France
Tel : (3) 3462-0852
Fax : (3) 3462-5406

Bice, Anita S.
1009 Park Avenue, Moody,
AL 35004, USA
Tel / Fax : (205) 640-6168

Bliss, Philip
22 Briggs Ave., Fairport NY 14450, USA
Tel / Fax : (716) 377-9771

Boatto, Guerrino
Via Monte Piana,
47 - 30171 Mestre - Venezia, Italy
Tel / Fax : (41) 926-580

Bressan, Davide
Via Marconi N. 1, Sacile (PN), 33077 Italy
Tel : (434) 781-850 / 781-065
Fax : (434) 781-850

Brown, Colin
11-12 Westgate Street, Bath Avon,
BA1 1EQ, England
Tel : (1225) 442-401
Fax : (1255) 446-674

Brunnick, Jeanne
1233 Hermosa Ave. STE 212
Hermosa Beach, CA 90254, USA
Tel : (310) 798-2771
Fax : (310) 798-2791

Busch, Lonnie
Airbusch Studio
15 North Gore, Suite 202,
St. Louis MO 63119, USA
Tel : (314) 962-7099
Fax : (314) 962-7659

Cafagna, Giuseppe
c/o Tranquilli Vittoria, Via Constantino 95,
00195 Rome, Italy

Cain, Thomas
510 Toluca Park Drive, Burbank,
CA 91505, USA
Tel : (818) 557-1305
Fax : (818) 246-4898

Calderon, Lee
150 Corona Avenue, Long Beach,
California 90803, USA
Tel / Fax : (310) 439-9216

Campbell, Philip H.
546 South Meridian Street,
Suite 511 Indianapolis 46225, USA
Tel : (317) 686-0895

Cariello, Maria Letizia
Via De Amicis, 47 - 20123 Milano, Italy
Tel : (2) 835-6502

Ceci Bartels Associates
3286 Ivanhoe, St Louis, MO 63139, USA
Tel : (314) 781-7377
Fax : (314) 781-8017

Chester, Celia
17 The Larneys, Kirby Cross,
Essex, Frinton-on-Sea, CO 130 UG, England
Tel : (1255) 679-223

Cicchetti, Daniela
Via G.ppe Chiarelli,10 - 00156,
Rome, Italy
Tel / Fax : (6) 411-5080

Clark, Peter
62 Morley Road, East Twickenham,
Middlesex TW1 2HF, England
Tel : (181) 892-0815
Fax : (181) 891-6057

Clark, Tim
1256, 25th Street, Santa Monica,
CA 90404, USA
Tel : (310) 453-7613
Fax : (310) 828-9430

Clauson, Thierry
27, Rue Pes Eaux-Vives,
CH1207 Geneve, Switzerland
Tel / Fax : (22) 736-6510

Colbert, Anthony
2 Stream Cottage, Staunton-On-Arrow,
NR. Leominster, Hereford HR6 9HR,
England
Tel : (1544) 388-327
Fax : (1544) 267-027

Conca, Germana
Via General Govone 57,
20155 Milano, Italy
Tel / Fax : (2) 3310-4332

Conlin, Stephen
69 Ridgmount Gardens,
London WC1E 7AX, Enlgand
Tel : (171) 580-9818
Fax : (171) 580 -9493

Culic, Ned
90 Clyde Street, St. Kilda,
Melbourne 3182, Australia
Tel : (3) 534-6445
Fax : (3) 534-6394

Custodio, Bernard
20103 Baltar Street,
Canoga Park, CA 91306, USA
Tel : (818) 998-4242
Fax : (818) 708-0158

D'Altan, Paolo
Superstudio 13, Via P. Forcella,
13-20144 Milano, Italy
Tel / Fax : (2) 5180-2001

David Goldman Agency
41 Union Square West, Suite 918,
NY 10003, USA
Tel : (212) 807-6627
Fax : (212) 463-8175

Davies, Tim
Big Road Blue Studio
66 A, Elm Park Road, Finchley,
London N3 1EB, England
Tel : (181) 349-3087
Fax : (181) 349-2026

De Muth, Roger
4103 Chenango St., Cazenovia,
NY 13035, USA
Tel / Fax : (315) 655-8599

Detwiler, Darius
Artists' Rep : Dick Washington
22727 Cielo Vista, San Antonio,
Texas 78255, USA
Tel : (210) 698-1409
Fax : (210) 698-1603

[DE-VI-ZU] Images Publiques
Artist Rep : Peter Bertoux / John D. Price
217 Rue Lafayette, 75010 Paris, France
Tel : (1) 4209-6346
Fax : (1) 4209-6333

Diez-Luckie, Catherine
6910 Jarvis Ave, Newark CA 94560, USA
Tel / Fax : (510) 713-2400

Durk, James A.
1853 Hastings Avenue, Downers Grove,
IL 60516, USA
Tel / Fax : (800) 550-0444

Edgeley, Peter
Peter Edgeley Pty Ltd
Suite 17, 30 Queens Lane,
Melbourne 3004, Australia
Tel : (3) 9866-6620
Fax : (3) 9866-6621

Ellis, Max
22 Thorney Hedge Road, Chiswick,
London W4 5SD, England
Tel : (181) 995-4771
Fax : (181) 742-7391

Evangelista, Mauro
Contrada S.M. delle Vergini,
62100 Macerata, Italy
Tel / Fax : (733) 736-723

Fast, Ingo
25 Broadway, Brooklyn, NY 11211, USA
Tel / Fax : (718) 387-9570

Faerber, Kevin
53 Beak Street, London W1R 3LF, England
Tel : (171) 287-1732
Fax : (171) 437-4836

Favero, Constanza
Via Tanaro, 3 - 20020 Lainate, Milano, Italy
Tel / Fax : (2) 9325-7043

Folco, Monica Di
Via Buggiano 49, 00148 Rome, Italy
Tel : (6) 653-7498

Fox, John
Sudbury House, 4 Tylney Road,
Bromley BR1 2RP, England
Tel : (181) 466-0655
Fax : (181) 466-6610

Garden Studio
Artist Rep: John Havergal
23 Ganton Street, London W1V 1LA, England
Tel : (171) 287-9191
Fax : (171) 287-9131

Garrity, Bruce
249 S, Broad Street,
Penns Grove, NJ 08069, USA
Tel : (609) 299-3966
Fax : (609) 299-7818

Gazzoni, Alessandra
V.le Monte Nero, 48 - 20135 Milano, Italy
Tel : (2) 546-6176

Giacon, Massimo
Via Marchetto Da Padova 31 - 35100,
Padova, Italy
Tel : (49) 750-845

Giandelli, Gabriella
Via Fiuggi 37, 20159 Milano, Italy
Tel / Fax : (2) 6900-3362

Giuseppe, Di Dio
Via Cappuccini 25 - 26013 Crema (CR), Italy
Tel : (3) 733-0020

Gosfield, Joshua
200 Varick Street #508, NY 10014, USA
Tel / Fax : (212) 645-8826

Gudynas, Bernard
59 Neville Road, Stoke Newington,
London N16 8SW, England
Tel / Fax : (171) 923-3618

Gudynas, Peter
89 Hazelwell Crescent, Stirchley,
Birmingham, B30 2QE, England
Tel / Fax : (121) 459-0080

Gurvin, Abe
31341 Holly Drive, Laguna Beach,
CA 92677, USA
Tel / Fax : (714) 499-2001

Harrington, Glenn
329 Twin Lear Road, Pipersville,
PA 18947, USA
Tel / Fax : (610) 294-8104

Harrison, Stuart
Cabin D, Clarendon Buildings,
11 Ronalds Road, Highbury,
London N5-1XL, England
Tel : (171) 241-3230
Fax : (171) 609-3918

Hayashi, Hirotaka
1-4-8-101 Izumi, Suginami-ku,
Tokyo 168, Japan
Tel / Fax : (3) 3323-0145

Holmberg, Irmeli (Artist Rep)
280 Madison Avenue, Suite 1010,
NY 10016, USA
Tel : (212) 545-9155
Fax : (212) 545-9462

Hurley, Gregory M.
5051 Rimers Drive,
Jackson MI 49201, USA
Tel : (517) 563-2096

Irilli,Silvio
Via Vittorio Veneto, 51 - 14019 ,
Villanova D'Asti-Asti
Tel / Fax : (141) 948-625

Isip, Jordin
44 4th Place Apartment 2, Brooklyn,
NY 11231, USA
Tel : (718) 624-6538
Fax : (718) 624-1994

Janice Stefanski Represents
2022 Jones Street,
San Francisco, CA 94133, USA
Tel : (415) 928-0457
Fax : (415) 775-6337

Julià, Carme
Mercedes, 10, 08024 Barcelona, Spain
Tel / Fax : (3) 210-7406

Kann, Victoria
336 E., 22nd Street #3R,
NY 10010, USA
Tel / Fax : (212) 979-0988

Kessler, Mario
AGD, Am Eichet 12A,
8913 Schondorf, Germany
Fax : (49) 8192-7053

Knepper, Mike
Beerentaltritt 111,
21077 Hamburg, Germany
Tel : (40) 792-2028
Fax : (40) 790-9556

Kunz, Anita
230 Ontario Street, Toronto,
Ontario M5A 2V5, Canada
Tel : (416) 364-3846
Fax : (416) 368-3947

Lane, Kim
59 Earlsbrook Road, Redhill,
Surrey RH1 6DR, England
Tel / Fax : (1737) 760-513

Langford, Frank
93 The Ridgeway, Cuffley, Herts,
EN6 4BG, England
Tel / Fax : (1707) 872-015

Lessard, Marie
4641 Hutchison, Montreal,
Quebec H2V 4A2, Canada
Tel / Fax : (514) 272-5696

Ling, Maggie
104A Highbury Park,
London N5 2XE, England
Tel : (171) 3599-0479
Fax : (171) 359-6869

Liogier, Vikki
12 Brenda Road (off Mandrake Road)
London SW17 7DB, England
Tel / Fax : (181) 682 0780

Lowe, Vicky
281 Sandycombe Road, Kew,
Richmond, Surrey TW9 3LU, England
Tel / Fax : (181) 948 -6741

Machalek, Jan
3355 / 108 Queen Mary Road,
Montreal, Quebec H3V 1A5, Canada
Tel : (514) 341-1532

M.A.D.
Patricia McShane / Erik Adigard
P.O. Box 190 Sausalito,
CA 94966, USA
Tel : (415) 331-1023
Fax : (415) 331-1034

Malgaroli, Maria Luisa
Via Matteotti 9, Rodano 20090
Milano, Italy
Tel : (2) 953-2098
Fax : (2) 9532-0489

Manning, Lisa
12 Ledge Lane, Gloucester,
MA 01930, USA
Tel : (508) 281-3983

Marchegiani, Gioia
Via F.B. Rastrelli n. 135,
00128, Rome, Italy
Tel : (6) 507-0685

Marion Moskowitz Represents, Inc.
315 East 68th Street,
NY 10021, USA
Tel / Fax : (212) 517-4919

Mattingly, David B.
1112 Bloomfield Street,
Hoboken, NJ 07030, USA
Tel : (201) 659-7404
Fax : (201) 656-3092

Mazzetti, Alan
834 Moultrie Street, San Francisco,
CA 94110, USA
Tel / Fax : (415) 647-7677

Meganck, Robert
Communication Design Inc.
1 North 5th Street, Suite 500,
Richmond, Virginia 23219, USA
Tel : (804) 644-9200
Fax : (804) 644-1045

Minichiello, Mario
61 Scotland Road, Little Bowden,
Market Harborough LE16 8AY, England
Tel / Fax : (1858) 431-456

Moran, Mike
24 Clifton Park Road,
Bristol BS8 3HL, England
Tel : (44) 272-731673

Morel, Frederic
12 rue Bodin, 69001-Lyon, France
Tel : (78) 395-085

Neubecker, Robert
c/o Brigham Young University,
Provo UTAH 84602, USA
Tel : (801) 649-2232
Fax : (801) 645-8898

Ogden, Michael
2 Carnarvon Road, Redland,
Bristol BS6 7DP, England
Tel : (117) 924-8376

Olschewski, Anja
Heinsbergstr 19, D-50674 Köln, Germany
Tel : (221) 240-5244
Fax : (220) 421 308

Otnes, Fred
26 Chalburn Road, West Redding,
CT 06896, USA
Tel : (203) 938-2829
Fax : (203) 431-4983

Otto, Dettmer E.
26 Brunswick Place, Hove,
East Sussex BN3 1NA, England
Tel : (1273) 722-015
Fax : (1273) 722-666

Palmer, Christopher
Pen Point Productions
7336 S. Blackstone Ave,
Chicago IL 60619, USA
Tel / Fax : (312) 684-3753

Pastor, Terry
Kesmark House, Gooseberry Hill,
Swanton Morley, Norfolk,
NR20 4PD, England
Tel / Fax : (136) 263-7663

Petrone, Valeria
Via Monviso, 35 - Milano, Italy
Tel / Fax : (2) 3360-5425

Phillips, Arthur
The Crow's Nest
2 Acre Road, Kingston-Upon-Thames,
Surrey KT2 6EF, England
Tel : (181) 547-3299
Fax : (181) 541-3732

Pijak, Peter
Wildpfad 14a, D-51503
Rösrath/Hoffnungsthal, Germany
Tel : (2205) 86633
Fax : (221) 763-070

Plikat, Ari
Steinmetz Strasse13,
D-44143 Dortmund, Germany
Tel : (231) 515-227
Fax : (231) 515-917

Primerano, Roberta
V.le E. Franceschini, 100 - 00155,
Rome, Italy
Tel / Fax : (6) 407-0275

Reactor Art & Design Ltd
51 Camden Street, Toronto,
Ontario M5V 1V2, Canada
Tel : (416) 703-1913
Fax : (416) 703-6556

Reppel, Aletha
905 West 29 Street, Austin,
Texas 78705, USA
Tel : (512) 478-0853
Fax : (512) 478-5123

Ricci, Stefano
Via Demetrio Martinelli 10,
40133 Bologna, Italy
Tel / Fax : (51) 387-197

Roberts, Liz
7 Bedford Grove, Eastbourne,
East Sussex, BN21 2DT, England
Tel : (1323) 732-953
Fax : (1323) 430-223

Rogers, Lilla
6 Parker Road, Arlington, MA 02174, USA
Tel : (617) 641-2787
Fax : (617) 641- 2244

Rogers, Paul
12 South Fair Oaks 202,
Pasadena CA 91105, USA
Tel : (818) 564-8728
Fax : (818) 564-8729

Roseler, Peter
Mariengarten 15,
48282 Emsdetten, Germany
Tel / Fax : (25) 723-637

Rossino, Michelangelo
Via San Quintino, 23 - 10121 Torino, Italy
Tel / Fax : (11) 549-063

Roy, Joanna
549 West 123rd Street, NY 10027, USA
Tel / Fax : (212) 663-7876

CALL FOR ENTRIES

Should you be interested in being included in the Index, we would ask you to send us a representative selection of your recent work in the form of transparencies or photographs suitable for reproduction, to enable us to select works we wish to use in the publication. **The deadline for entries for the 1996 Index is 15 November 1995.** We will, of course, also require all the relevant information which will accompany each work, e.g. title, year, client, etc. Please do not send us originals. The publication of your work in the Index will be free of charge to you. Your name and address will be listed in the book. We would ask you to sign and return the contract along with your submission for the publication to us at the address below.

TERMS AND CONDITIONS FOR PUBLICATION OF MATERIALS SUPPLIED TO THE PUBLISHER BY THE ARTIST FOR INCLUSION IN THE INDEX.

1. The Artist grants and assigns the Publisher (Page One Publishing Pte Ltd) the right to publish the work submitted by the artist in the Index without limitation in quantity and in any size and for an unlimited period of time.

2. The Publisher has the right to have the published Index sold in any country, without geographical limitation. The right to publish the work is non-exclusive.

3. The Publisher may refuse to reproduce any submitted entry, transparency or photograph, which he feels is unsuitable for publication in the Index.

4. The Publisher will not be responsible for printing discrepancies, for damage to or loss of any material supplied, howsoever this may arise, nor for any delay in publishing, or omission to publish any accepted submission.

5. Submitted material will become the property of the Publisher. It may be returned to the Artist on demand and at the expense of the Artist.

6. The Artist represents and warrants that he is the sole and exclusive proprietor of all materials submitted by him to the Publisher, whether transparencies, photographs, copies or other, and that the inclusion of these in the Index will not infringe upon any existing copyright or other proprietary right; he further guarantees that these materials will not contain matter which is objectionable, obscene, defamatory, or in breach of the peace and good morals of any other law or regulation.

7. The Artist further guarantees that he shall hold the Publisher harmless against any claim against the Publisher by a third party arising out of the materials submitted by him to the Publisher.

8. Notwithstanding the acceptance of material for incorporation in the Index, the Publisher reserves the right, at any time, not to publish, to discontinue publication, or to modify it (e.g. enlarge or reduce in size, bleed edges, use details, cut out). The Publisher rejects all responsibility for the non-appearance of documents or reproduction, whatever the cause might be.

9. The materials may only be used for Index publications and any advertisement, brochure or other printed matter produced specifically for the purpose of promoting the sale of these publications.

PLEASE FILL OUT AND ATTACH TO EACH ENTRY.

Title of image:

Art Director:

Designer:

Illustrator, Photographer, Stylist

Agency, Studio:

Client, Publisher:

Description of assignment/other information:

Signature:

I hereby grant Page One Publishing Pte Ltd non-exclusive permission for use of the submitted material, for which I have full reproduction rights.

Agreed by (Artist):   Countersigned by (Publisher):
                             Page One Publishing Pte Ltd

Name:

Address:

Date:

Page One Publishing Pte Ltd, attn.: Violet Tan, Block 4, Pasir Panjang Road, # 06-35 Alexandra Distripark, Singapore 0511

EINLADUNG ZUR TEILNAHME

Sollten Sie daran interessiert sein, in den Index aufgenommen zu werden, bitten wir Sie, uns eine repräsentative Auswahl Ihrer letzten Arbeiten in Form von reproduktionsfähigen Diapositiven oder Fotos zu übersenden, damit wir diejenigen Arbeiten auswählen können, die wir in der Publikation verwenden möchten. **Letzter Einsendetermin für den Index 1996 ist der 15. November 1995.** Wir benötigen natürlich auch alle relevanten Informationen im Zusammenhang mit den einzelnen Arbeiten, z.B. Titel, Jahr, Kunde u.s.w. Bitte schicken Sie uns keine Originale. Die Veröffentlichung Ihrer Arbeiten im Index ist für Sie kostenlos. Ihr Name und Ihre Anschrift werden im Buch genannt. Bitte unterzeichnen Sie den Vertrag und reichen Sie ihn zusammen mit Ihrem Bildmaterial an die unten angegebene Adresse ein.

BESTIMMUNGEN UND BEDINGUNGEN ZUR VERÖFFENTLICHUNG VON MATERIALIEN, DIE DER KÜNSTLER DEM HERAUSGEBER ZUR AUFNAHME IN DEN INDEX ZUR VERFÜGUNG GESTELLT HAT.

1. Der Künstler gewährt dem Herausgeber (Page One Publishing Pte Ltd) und überträgt auf diesen das Recht zur Veröffentlichung der von ihm eingereichten Arbeiten im Index, und zwar ohne mengenmäßige Beschränkung, in jeder beliebigen Größe und auf unbegrenzte Zeit.

2. Der Herausgeber ist berechtigt, den veröffentlichten Index in jedem beliebigen Land – ohne geographische Einschränkung – verkaufen zu lassen. Das Recht zur Veröffentlichung der Arbeiten ist nicht ausschließlich.

3. Der Herausgeber kann die Reproduktion eingereichter Arbeiten (Diapositive oder Fotos) ablehnen, wenn er der Meinung ist, daß diese sich nicht für eine Veröffentlichung im Index eignen.

4. Der Herausgeber haftet nicht für auf den Druck zurückzuführende Abweichungen, für Schäden an oder Verlust von eingereichten Materialien (gleichgültig auf welche Weise diese entstehen), für Verzögerungen bei der Veröffentlichung oder die Unterlassung der Veröffentlichung angenommener Einsendungen.

5. Eingereichte Materialien gehen in das Eigentum des Herausgebers über. Sie können auf Anfrage und auf Kosten des Künstlers an diesen zurückgesandt werden.

6. Der Künstler erklärt und garantiert, daß er der einzige und ausschließliche Eigentümer aller durch ihn an den Herausgeber gesandten Materialien ist,

und zwar unabhängig davon, ob es sich bei diesen Materialien um Diapositive, Fotografien, Kopien oder sonstige Materialien handelt, und daß durch die Aufnahme derselben in den Index keinerlei bestehendes Copyright oder sonstiges Eigentumsrecht verletzt wird; weiterhin garantiert er, daß diese Materialien nichts enthalten, was anstößig, obszön oder beleidigend ist bzw. die öffentliche Sicherheit gefährdet oder gegen die sittlichen Grundsätze sonstiger Gesetze oder Vorschriften verstößt.

7. Darüber hinaus garantiert der Künstler, daß er den Herausgeber von allen durch einen Dritten an ihn gerichteten Ansprüchen freistellt, soweit letztere auf dem dem Herausgeber durch den Künstler überlassenen Materialien beruhen.

8. Der Herausgeber behält sich das Recht vor, unbeschadet der Annahme von Materialien zur Einbeziehung in den Index zu jedem beliebigen Zeitpunkt keine Veröffentlichung vorzunehmen bzw. die Veröffentlichung einzustellen oder sie abzuändern (z.B. Vergrößerung oder Verkleinerung, Beschnitt, Verwendung von Ausschnitten und Freistellungen). Unabhängig vom Grund für das Nichterscheinen von Dokumenten oder Reproduktionen lehnt der Herausgeber jede Haftung für das Nichterscheinen derselben ab.

9. Die Materialien dürfen ausschließlich für Index-Publikationen und Werbeanzeigen, Broschüren oder sonstige Drucksachen verwendet werden, die speziell zum Zwecke der Verkaufsförderung für diese Publikationen hergestellt werden.

BITTE AUSFÜLLEN UND AN JEDE EINGESANDTE ARBEIT HEFTEN.

Bildtitel:

Art Director:

Designer:

Illustrator, Fotograf, Stylist:

Agentur, Studio:

Kunde, Herausgeber:

Beschreibung des Auftrags/sonstige Informationen:

Unterschrift:
Hiermit erteile ich Page One Publishing Pte Ltd die nicht ausschließliche Genehmigung zur Verwendung der eingereichten Materialien, für die ich über alle Reproduktionsrechte verfüge.

Einverstanden (Künstler):   Gegengezeichnet durch (Herausgeber): Page One Publishing Pte Ltd

Name:

Anschrift:

Datum:

Page One Publishing Pte Ltd, z. H. Violet Tan, Block 4, Pasir Panjang Road, # 06-35 Alexandra Distripark, Singapore 0511

DEMANDE DE PARTICIPATION

Si vous êtes intéressé par la figuration de vos œuvres dans l'index, nous vous prions de nous envoyer une sélection représentative des plus récentes sous forme de diapositives ou de photographies faciles à reproduire pour nous permettre de sélectionner les ouvrages que nous aimerions utiliser dans la publication. **La date limite d'inscription pour l'index 1996 est le 15 novembre 1995.** Il est évident que nous aurons également besoin de toutes les informations importantes spécifiques à chacune des œuvres, par ex. le titre, l'année, le client, etc. Nous vous prions de ne pas nous envoyer d'originaux. La publication de votre œuvre dans l'index sera gratuite. Votre nom et votre adresse seront indiqués dans le livre. Nous vous prions de nous retourner le contrat signé avec votre œuvre soumise.

MODALITES DE PUBLICATION D'OUVRAGES FOURNIS PAR L'ARTISTE A L'EDITEUR EN VUE DE SON INSERTION DANS L'INDEX.

1. L'artiste octroie et cède à l'éditeur (Page One Publishing Pte Ltd) le droit de publier dans l'index l'œuvre soumise par lui-même sans aucune restriction quant à la quantité et la taille et pour une période illimitée.

2. L'éditeur a le droit de vente de l'index publié dans n'importe quel pays, sans aucune limitation géographique. Le droit de publier l'œuvre est un droit non-exclusif.

3. L'éditeur peut refuser de reproduire une œuvre soumise, diapositive ou photographie, s'il la juge inappropriée à la publication dans l'index.

4. L'éditeur ne sera responsable ni d'éventuels défauts d'impression, endommagement ou perte du matériel remis, ni d'un retard de publication ou de l'omission de la publication d'une œuvre acceptée.

5. Le matériel soumis deviendra la propriété de l'éditeur. Il pourra être renvoyé à l'artiste sur sa demande et à ses frais.

6. L'artiste déclare et garantit être le propriétaire unique et exclusif de tout le matériel soumis par lui-même à l'éditeur, qu'il s'agisse de diapositives, photographies, copies ou autres, et que son inclusion dans l'index n'enfreindra pas de droit d'auteur déjà existant ou autre droit de propriété; il garantit d'autre part que ce matériel ne contient aucun sujet choquant, obscène, diffamatoire ou portant atteinte à l'ordre public et à la bonne moralité de toute loi ou réglementation.

7. L'artiste garantit en outre qu'il tiendra l'éditeur à couvert contre toute plainte portée contre celui-ci par une tierce personne suite au matériel remis par lui-même à l'éditeur.

8. Malgré l'acceptation du matériel pour son enregistrement dans l'index, l'éditeur se réserve à tout instant le droit de ne pas procéder à la publication, d'interrompre la publication ou de la modifier (par ex. agrandissement ou réduction, changement du pourtour, utilisation de détails, découpe de certaines parties). L'éditeur rejette toute responsabilité pour la non-parution de documents ou de reproductions, quelle qu'en soit la raison.

9. Le matériel remis ne pourra être utilisé qu'à des fins de publication dans l'index, à des fins publicitaires, pour une brochure ou autre imprimé spécialement réalisé dans le but de promouvoir la vente de ces publications.

A REMPLIR ET ATTACHER A CHAQUE ŒUVRE SOUMISE.

Titre:

Directeur artistique:

Créateur:

Illustrateur, photographe, styliste:

Agence, atelier:

Client, éditeur:

Description de la cession des droits et obligations/Autres informations:

Signature:

Par la présente, je soussigné accorde à l'éditeur One Publishing Pte Ltd l'autorisation non-exclusive d'user du matériel soumis pour lequel je suis seul détenteur des droits de reproduction.

Approuvé par (artiste):

Contresigné par (éditeur):
Page One Publishing Pte Ltd

Nom:

Adresse:

Date:

INVITACION A PARTICIPAR

Si le interesa ser incluido en nuestro índice, envíenos una selección representativa de sus trabajos más recientes, ya sea en forma de diapositivas, o como fotografías aptas para reproducir, de tal modo que podamos seleccionar sus trabajos para emplearlos en nuestra publicación. **La fecha límite para el registro en el directorio de 1996 es el 15 de noviembre de 1995.** Para tal fin precisamos, por supuesto, la información más destacada sobre cada trabajo, por ejemplo, el año, el cliente, etc. Por favor no nos envíe originales. La publicación de sus trabajos en el directorio será totalmente gratuita para Ud. Su nombre y dirección serán listados en el libro. Posteriormente le solicitaremos que firme y nos remita de vuelta el contrato con el material suministrado.

TÉRMINOS Y CONDICIONES PARA LA PUBLICACIÓN DE MATERIALES SUMINISTRADOS POR EL ARTISTA AL EDITOR PARA SER INCLUIDOS EN EL DIRECTORIO (INDEX).

1. El artista concede y adjudica al editor (Page One Publishing Pte Ltd) los derechos para publicar en el directorio los trabajos suministrados por el artista, sin limitación de cantidad ni de tamaño y por un período indefinido de tiempo.

2. El editor tiene el derecho de venta del directorio en cualquier país, sin limitación geográfica. El derecho a la publicación del trabajo es de no exclusividad.

3. El editor rehusará reproducir cualquier trabajo, diapositiva o fotografía autorizadas que considere no conveniente para su inclusión en el directorio.

4. El editor no será responsable de discrepancias en la impresión, de la pérdida o del daño del material suministrado, sin importar la causa, como tampoco de cualquier demora en la publicación, o de omitir la publicación de cualquier trabajo propuesto y aceptado.

5. El material que haya sido autorizado se convertirá en propiedad del editor. Dicho material podrá ser devuelto a solicitud y por cuenta del artista.

6. El artista declara y garantiza que es el único y exclusivo propietario de todos los materiales suministrados por su parte al editor, ya se trate de diapositivas, fotografías, copias u otros, y que la inclusión de éstos en el directorio no infringirá derechos de autor existentes o propiedad intelectual alguna. Además, el artista garantiza que dicho material no incluirá temas censurables, obscenos, difamatorios o que vayan en contra de la moral y de la paz o de cualquier ley o regulación.

7. El artista garantiza, además, la inmunidad del editor en caso de reclamo por parte de terceros contra el editor, que se presente a causa del material autorizado al editor por el artista.

8. No obstante la aceptación del material para su inclusión en el directorio, el editor se reserva el derecho de, en cualquier momento, no publicar, suspender la publicación o de modificarla (p. ej. aumentando o reduciendo el tamaño, los márgenes, utilizando detalles o fragmentos). El editor no asume responsabilidad alguna por la no aparición de documentos o por la reproducción, cualquiera que sea la causa para ello.

9. Los materiales sólo podrán ser utilizados para publicarse en el directorio, o en anuncios, folletos u otros medios impresos producidos específicamente con el fin de promover la venta de estas publicaciones.

- -

POR FAVOR, RELLENAR Y PEGAR EN CADA TRABAJO ENVIADO.

Título:

Director artístico:

Diseñador:

Ilustrador, fotógrafo, estilista:

Agencia, estudio:

Cliente, editor:

Descripción de la cesión de derechos y obligaciones/ otras informaciones:

Firma:

Por la presente concedo a Page One Publishing Pte Ltd autorización no exclusiva para utilizar el material propuesto, sobre el cual poseo los plenos derechos de reproducción.

Aprobado por (artista):   Refrendado por (el editor):
Page One Publishing Pte Ltd

Nombre:

Dirección:

Fecha:

Page One Publishing Pte Ltd, p/e a Violet Tan, Block 4, Pasir Panjang Road, # 06-35 Alexandra Distripark, Singapore 0511